Aspects of Transition to Market Economies in Eastern Europe

ULRICH THIESSEN

Avebury

Aldershot • Brookfield USA • Hong Kong • Singapore • Sydney

Published by
Avebury
Ashgate Publishing Limited
Gower House
Croft Road
Aldershot
Hants GU11 3HR
England

Ashgate Publishing Company
Old Post Road
Brookfield
Vermont 05036
USA

Typeset by
Kathleen Fedouloff
44 Rosemont Road
London W3 9LY
081-993 8258

British Library Cataloguing in Publication Data
Thiessen, Ulrich
    Aspects of Transition to Market Economies
    in Eastern Europe
    I. Title
    338.947

ISBN 1 85628 679 7

Printed and Bound in Great Britain by
Athenaeum Press Ltd, Newcastle upon Tyne.

Contents

Tables and figures

Abbreviations

BIS   = Bank for International Settlements

BNB   = National Bank of Bulgaria

CNB   = National Bank of the Czech Republic

CMEA = Council for Mutual Economic Assistance

EC   = European Communities

NBH   = National Bank of Hungary

NBP   = National Bank of Poland

NBS   = National Bank of the Slovakia

IMF   = International Monetary Fund

OECD = Organization for Economic Cooperation and Development

Preface

The papers contained in this volume were prepared for the European I Department of the International Monetary Fund. The author wishes to thank Gerard Bélanger, Biswajit Banerjee, Ayai Chopra, Eric Clifton, Burckard Drees, Maryanne Mrakovcic, Mark Lutz, Mark Stone, and Tessa van der Willigen for their generous support and Aline Clark for her secretarial assistance. Errors are the responsibility of the author. The views expressed should not be attributed to the International Monetary Fund.

Part One
INCOMES POLICY

1 Introduction

Unemployment in Eastern European countries has risen steadily since stabilization and restructuring programs were implemented following the disintegration of the Soviet Union and collapse of Soviet trade. Owing to the extent of adverse shocks and indexation of nominal wages to consumer price levels, adjustment of aggregate real wage levels lagged behind the path that would have been required to maintain a level of high employment. This paper focuses on the five Eastern European countries Bulgaria, the Czech and Slovak Federal Republic,[1] the Republic of Hungary, the Republic of Poland, and Romania. Median unemployment in the five countries climbed to 8 per cent of the labour force in 1991 and an estimated 11.6 per cent in 1992. Although the evolution of unemployment differs markedly among the countries, one fundamental question is: given the declines of real output in each of them since 1989 and slowly proceeding privatization, how can adjustment of the aggregate real wage level, required to maintain or increase employment, be facilitated so as to prevent a vicious cycle of nominal wage increases and subsequent reliance on inflation to adjust real wages to the feasible aggregate level. The role of incomes policy, advocated since long by prominent economists as a weapon against inflation and unemployment, particularly with regard to Western European countries whose labour markets tend to be characterized by pronounced rigidities, is assessed. The paper is organized as follows: Section 2 reviews the theoretical analysis of incomes policy. Section 3 summarizes the experiences industrial countries had with incomes policy during the past three decades. Section 4 examines the major macro- and microeconomic developments in the five countries before evaluating the adopted incomes policies in Section 5. Section 6 contains summary and concluding remarks.

2 Theoretical evidence

1. Incomes policy and the price mechanism

The term 'incomes policy' has come to represent a wide range of policies that aim at reducing the rate of wage and price inflation. If wages would rise, on average, in proportion to the average rise in labour productivity, measured in terms of output per man-hour then, *ceteris paribus*, there would be no pressure on the aggregate profit margin and wage inflation would not exist.[2] The poles of incomes policies are mild policies of moral suasion and complete price and wage controls. From a viewpoint of traditional theory of economic order, incomes policies ought to be distinguished into two types:[3] on the one hand, there are incomes policies that intend to influence growth of wage and price levels using measures that leave the price mechanism unhindered as the means to co-ordinate plans, but improve its functioning (anti-trust policies, taxes, subsidies, promotion of both market transparency and mobility of factors of production etc.).[4] On the other hand, there are incomes policies that affect the price mechanism's workings by providing a substitute for it and thus for market forces (controls, generalized guidelines, moral suasion policy in the form of recommended wage and price restraint etc.). In a market economy, there is, in principle, no justification for policies of the latter type. The reason is uncertainty about the allocational and distributional effects of direct interference with the price mechanism. In a market economy without elements of central planning, the price mechanism provides for total plan co-ordination (from a static as well as a dynamic point of view) and thus determines resource allocation, the income distribution, and provides for individual freedom in the sense that individuals' planning is not restricted except by laws securing mainly property rights and freedom to engage in contracts and compliance with contracts.[5] Since such a system tends to entail unsustainable developments (monopolization, skewed income distribution etc.), and therefore becomes unstable in the

4

long run, the above mentioned measures need to be employed to improve the functioning of the price mechanism.[6] Rather than referring to Walrasian equilibrium or the complete set of Arrow-Debreu markets, analyses of empirical examples of economies that experienced periods during which direct interference with the price mechanism was avoided may be called for. The effects on resource allocation and income distribution of indirect means are in general less far-reaching and therefore easier to forecast and trace than are welfare effects of direct interference. If it is accepted that policy measures whose welfare effects are not ascertainable to a reasonable degree should not be implemented, then interference with the price mechanism in a market economy will rarely occur. Consider the welfare effects resulting from imposition of effective wage and price controls: assuming that prices and wages are at their competitive levels, the immediate effects of these controls are shortages and possibly restrained competition. If prices and wages would be above competitive levels in the absence of controls and to the extent that the rent accrues, for instance, due to superior entrepreneurship (e.g. successfully implemented research), immediate shortages may not occur but the incentives to invest in activities directed at making the demand curve faced by a firm less elastic would be weakened. A second long run welfare loss occurs if price controls result in distorted relative prices and thus in allocative inefficiency. A third loss is given by the administrative costs of controls. Fourth, individual freedom is curtailed.[7] The magnitude and duration of these welfare losses are uncertain and so is whether they are outweighed by the welfare gain due to moderation of wage inflation. If such guidelines are imposed because it is believed that prices do not correspond to their level prevailing in a competitive environment, then the question arises why an institutional prerequisite of any market economy, anti-trust laws, or put positively, laws protecting competition, fail to achieve that. Hence, on account of this belief, improvements of laws securing competition are required and not regulations hindering the price mechanism.[8] If an economy has to adjust in response to shocks rendering the capital stock largely obsolete, the primary objective will be improvement of the capital stock so as to raise labour productivity and hence employment and the feasible aggregate real wage level. Since this built-up of the capital stock will occur according to relative prices expected by investors, an undistorted price system and hence low trade barriers would save resources in the long run, because production would be permitted to fully reflect the comparative advantages of the economy.[9] Hence a case could, in principle, be made only for an incomes policy that employs instruments which complement the price mechanism as the primary means to co-ordinate plans.

It may be argued that, with the exception of one case explained below, the recommendation of incomes policy contains errors of logic (Johnson, 1972). First, there is no price or wage for a clearly defined quality and amount of product or labour delivered to the purchaser under clearly defined transaction conditions and contingent obligations. Hence, a transaction has an infinite number of dimensions and the exchange of a given commodity quantity whose money value is fixed can be effected by varying all other dimensions than the price. Second, incomes policy is no substitute for restrictive fiscal or monetary policy: on the one hand, it impinges on allocative efficiency due to its impact on relative wages and prices. On the other hand, with monetary policy expansionary, economic agents must wish to hold the resulting higher real money supply, implying that, with initially given output, pressure on prices arises and thus on the effectiveness of incomes policy. If incomes policy withstands these pressures, the just mentioned other dimensions of a transaction will be varied before output would respond sufficiently to lower interest rates and thus catch up with that higher level of the real money supply. If both, fiscal and monetary policy are expansionary and assuming constant interest rates, it appears unreasonable to expect no pressure on prices, even if capacity is under-utilized. Under the optimistic assumption that pressure is mild, the rise in aggregate demand (concomitant with, perhaps, some output rise) will, however, tend to result in a deterioration of the balance of payments and the public debt to GDP ratio may increase. Further factors, as discussed in more detail in the following section, inevitably make the policy unsustainable, even if incomes policy was effective. The periods of controls during war times, sometimes referred to by proponents of incomes policy, do not appear to be able to serve as prove for the potential beneficial power of incomes policy: the primary reason for the substantial output growth during these periods was productivity growth due to the intensity of research and concentration of the labour force on efficiency gains. In addition, these periods witnessed spiralling debt to GDP ratios and a curtailment of individual freedom to an extent a society may not accept during peacetime. It would appear difficult to enforce productivity growth by an incomes policy decree. Productivity growth requires entrepreneurship, preconditions for which appear to be both a stable political environment and conservative demand management. Third, an attempt to stabilize the value of money regardless of the quantity neglects the law of supply and demand and will require further regulations. Fourth, incomes policy appears to be an attempt to shift responsibility of demand management to wage negotiating parties by calling on them to exert self-denying refusal to follow the market signals. It thus inherently contradicts the very foundation of a market economy. Market-based incomes policy attempts to avoid the third and fourth problem. However, the first and second one remain.

The workings of incomes policy can be seen considering a simple model of supply of and demand for labour in which real wages and employment adjust according to a given mechanism when the labour market is in disequilibrium. There are three channels through which equilibrium employment could be raised: a downward shift in labour demand through a rise in labour productivity (e.g. improved labour-management relations, less strike activity, improved capital stock); a downward shift in labour supply through modified wage

6

demands; improvements of the adjustment mechanism resulting in faster adjustment of real wages and/or employment. With the exclusion of technological progress, it is common to subsume all measures that work through these channels as incomes policy. However, in this paper, incomes policy is defined narrowly, as labour market policy that attempts to directly influence wage formation. These measures thus work through the second and third channel. Hence, the discussion is more focused, because policies or issues such as management-labour relations and organization of wage bargaining are not part of incomes policy. However, the latter are, as incomes policy is, labour market (supply side) policies.

2. Incomes policy in an open economy

Notwithstanding the above reasoning, the voluminous literature on incomes policy is characterized by substantial dissension among economists as to the welfare effects of incomes policy. Are there exceptions to the rule explained above? It appears the argumentation put forward by advocates of incomes policy may be reduced to two cases. The first case refers to stabilization when inertial inflation is a central feature.[10] Inertia arises due to inflationary expectations and/or indexation of contracts to past inflation. Inflationary bias of an economy is due, in turn, to accommodating monetary policy permitting the following potential properties of a market economy to result in rising prices: uncompetitive labour and product markets, growing government sectors which are less competitive, tax push inflation as public sector growth in excess of output growth results in a rise of tax rates and as trade unions bargain in real disposable income terms with little consideration given to social security contributions and the supply of public services. In the presence of inertia, an economy is prevented from shifting from a high inflationary equilibrium to a low one without incurring output losses and unemployment, since the real money supply will contract in the process. Even if all market participants agree on disinflation and have rational expectations, a downward shift of the (expectations augmented) 'Phillips' curve, without movement along the curve, appears unlikely, because a free-rider problem and prisoner's dilemma are present.[11] Hence there are information externalities and thus the case for government intervention is convincing so as to provide a temporary shock to price and wage expectations. Imposition of price, wage (incomes policy), and exchange rate regulations or even controls may achieve a break of inertia at relatively low costs. Dependent upon the credibility of adopted disinflationary policies, the empirical evidence shows that such controls may or may not succeed.[12] It may be noted that the case for incomes policy appears strongest in high inflationary episodes, because the benefits appear to greatly exceed the costs. The lower the level of inflation, the weaker tends the case to become: with the initial inflation level declining, the benefits of breaking inertia decrease while the potential costs of incomes policy, namely allocative distortions, inequities, administrative inefficiencies, and enforcement may not decline. Therefore, at a relatively low level of inflation, restrictive policies without incomes policy support may be called for, which, if implemented consistently, may influence expectations such that growth is subject to an immediate positive impact.

The second case for incomes policy refers to narrowing the long run gap between potential and actual output and thus to reducing unemployment by means of accommodated expansionary fiscal policy.[13] Some advocates of incomes policy pursue even more ambitious goals. It is claimed that high unemployment in many countries witnessed during the past two decades requires altering social institutions so as to mitigate distributional conflict and achieve a more stable, just, and efficient economy. A basic premise in the work of these advocates is that they perceive price increases as incorporating an adverse externality (a non-functional element) stemming from monopolistic competition on most markets so that firms limit output and workers limit entry into the labour market. Rather than attempting to improve the degree of competition, these representatives prefer a market-based incomes policy which would improve efficiency by bringing the economy closer to the state of perfect competition. Thus higher growth and higher employment are expected. Even though some proponents of incomes policy may not admit to advocate expansionary policies, they tend to reject both stabilization or reduction of the public debt to GNP ratio or of the fiscal deficit to GNP ratio, and adoption of monetary targeting which aims at stabilizing the rate of inflation at a moderate level through long run growth of the money supply (the definition of the chosen aggregate being less relevant) consistent with both long run growth of potential output and of velocity of that money supply. The question thus arises how this rejection may be compatible with non-expansionary policies. To corroborate their case, some advocates of incomes policy refer to the period of controls in the United States during 1940 to 1944 when output rose more than twofold and unemployment fell from 14.6 per cent to 1.2 per cent.

Since expansionary policies may result in both accelerated inflation and even adverse real effects, additional use of incomes policy is proposed so as to prevent these adverse impacts on inflation and the exchange rate.[14] Crucial to any proposition of incomes policy in this second case is the functioning of the labour market. If the labour market tends to be competitive then, barring the above mentioned problems, incomes policy would appear questionable, because supply and demand for labour tend to equilibrate, and aggregate supply would be rather inelastic with expansionary policy affecting prices and not output. A lowering of wages would cause excess demand for labour.[15] It would follow that before discussing adoption of a certain type of incomes policy, there may be a need to reflect on whether restoration of competition in the labour market is feasible. While recognizing that existing institutions such as trade unions, cer-

8

tain constraints on employers, and income protecting programs raised social welfare, this would then lead to examination of potential measures available to improving competition.[16] If such improvement appears excluded, there would be the argument that differences in labour-management relations and work organization patterns may explain differences in long run economic performance better than wage rigidities (Aoki, 1988). Hence, prior to recommending an incomes policy, there would also be a need to examine whether these relations could be improved. In addition, there is theoretical and empirical support for the hypothesis for the degree of coordination among both employers and trade unions to have a decisive influence on wage pressure, dependent, however, on coverage (Calmfors and Driffill, 1988, Jackman et. al., 1991). The better the quality of coordination, among both employers and trade unions, the less unemployment is 'required' for trade unions to realize that attempts to raise wages relative to the price level contribute to unemployment. Experience has shown that countries who have a centralized process of collective bargaining or relatively strong coordination among employers' federations (Austria, Germany, Japan, Portugal, Scandinavian countries, Switzerland) tend to have lower unemployment than countries where bargaining is decentralized (Belgium, Canada, France, Italy, Netherlands, Spain, United Kingdom, United States).[17] Thus, important factors contributing to an alignment of growth of wages and labour productivity may be seen in labour-management relations and the system of wage bargaining a country adopts. It may also be noted that only long term unemployment constitutes a serious problem. If a high unemployment rate was known to be made up entirely of short term unemployment, this could be read as an indication of the economy's adaptability to continuously changing supply and demand conditions.

While the above reasoning applies to both a closed and open economy, analysis of incomes policy in the latter requires to consider interrelations between the tradeables and nontradeables sector, on the one hand, and a feedback mechanism between the external current account and incomes policy, on the other. Assuming non-competitiveness of the labour market as given, resulting in long term unemployment, and assuming improvements of both management-labour relations and the system of wage bargaining to be excluded, how may the macroeconomic and welfare effects of an incomes policy be ascertained? As explained below (Section 4), the considered five Eastern European countries maintain a high degree of openness with relatively low trade barriers and either pegged or managed floating exchange rate systems. Hence, the cases of an open economy with fixed and flexible exchange rates need to be distinguished.

With regard to the short run, if the exchange rate is fixed, the slope of the 'Phillips' curve tends to be relatively small, since price setting in the tradeables sector constraints increases of the overall price level. Assuming a balance of payments equilibrium is disturbed, for instance, due to expansionary policies or wage growth in excess of productivity growth, upward pressure on the price

9

level arises with firms in the tradeables sector loosing competitiveness. To the extent that domestic inflation exceeds that of international competitors, unemployment may result with a lag, possibly exacerbated if resources shift to the more profitable non-tradeables sector. Credibility of the fixed exchange rate policy would be a crucial factor in this process: if credibility is given, wage negotiating parties may consider competitiveness more readily.[18] If they do not find the exchange rate credible and the government adheres to the prevailing rate, the balance of payments will tend to deteriorate. In the short run, deviations from long run purchasing power parity may be sustainable, dependent upon the level of international reserves and capital flows. Proponents of incomes policy may see a development of deteriorating external competitiveness as providing a case for incomes policy. The experiences of several European economies with a high degree of openness, reviewed in Section 3, suggest, however, that incomes policy measures may result in further such steps with a government becoming increasingly involved in negotiations with wage bargaining parties, forced to make tax concessions in exchange for wage and price restraint which could result in additional distortions and inconsistent economic policies. Moreover, improvement of the balance of payments through incomes policy requires supplementary measures deflating domestic demand: in response to regained international competitiveness, the open sector requires additional resources which have to be shifted from the sheltered sector. Wage and price restraint is theoretically insufficient (Johnson, 1972). But even if policies regain the previous levels of international competitiveness and employment, the question arises what prevents the same adverse development from occurring in future. Permanent wage and price restraint through incomes policy as defined in this paper proved empirically infeasible, for many reasons (as reviewed below), the fundamental one being that either one of the wage negotiating parties perceived the resulting income distribution as imposed and unfair.

Under a flexible exchange rate system, the 'Phillips' curve tends to be steeper, because depreciation in response to domestic price increases would prevent a loss of competitiveness. Demand management (through monetary policy) tends to be relatively effective. Assuming the same disturbance noted above, trade unions and employers could regard depreciation as a remedy, providing a case for incomes policy in the view of its proponents so as to prevent a cycle of wage inflation and depreciations. The question arises again as to the sustainability of incomes policy. In several countries there has been a cycle of incomes policy measures, causing distortions and resulting in prolonged negotiations which may have contributed to a loss of resources for productive purposes.

Dependent on expectations formation, a certain time horizon is required for the 'Phillips' curve to become vertical. Inflation is then not an instrument available to influence unemployment. However, if, in the long run, growth of real output and employment are a negative function of inflation, causing a somewhat positively sloped long run 'Phillips' curve (Figure 2.1), knowledge of the

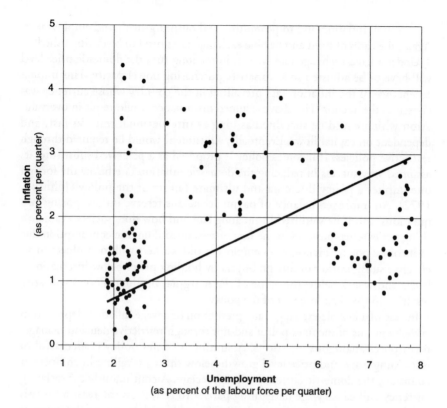

Unweighted average of 23 industrial countries' quarterly rate of change of the consumer price index regressed against a constant and the unweighted average rate of unemployment during the first quarter of 1960 and the fourth quarter of 1990.

Sources: International Monetary Fund, International Financial Statistics;
Organization for Economic Cooperation and Development,
Analytical Database

Figure 2.1   Industrial countries: long-run 'Phillips' curve, 1960-1990

wage and price equation would nevertheless be important, because their independent variables may enter the reaction function of the institution who controls growth of base money.[19] To the extent that decisions of the authority controlling base money take the wage and price equation as given and respond to their behavioral content, rather than attempt to influence it, market-based incomes policy could be called for so as to lowering long run wage inflation and thus overall inflation and to promoting real output growth and employment. Again, the cases of fixed and flexible exchange rates need to be distinguished.

Under a fixed exchange rate system, in the long run, the domestic price level will have to be adjusted so as to satisfy purchasing power parity. This implies acceptance of the inflation rate prevailing in the country whose currency was chosen as the anchor. The above assumed disturbance would result in overvaluation which could be sustained as long as international reserves last, and dependent on capital flows. Eventually, adjustment would be required through restrictive policies. If incomes policy is proposed as a perceived substitute, its assumed very success in reducing the domestic inflation rate below the foreign one implies a policy dilemma and ultimate failure of the policy (Johnson, 1972). An improved balance of payments means reserve inflow, posing two questions: can it be sterilized in the long run and how does society evaluate a rising net external position in the face of restrained domestic consumption due to incomes policy? Hence, both employers and workers will soon object to an effective subsidization of foreign buyers by holding prices below international levels and wages below the value of the marginal product. Forces will arise resulting in the abandonment of the policy.

In case of a flexible exchange rate, prevention of a wage inflation-depreciation cycle by means of incomes policy and not through restrictive demand management poses analogous questions. Assuming incomes policy is successful in restraining wage and price level growth below those prevailing in competitor countries, the domestic currency will appreciate. A continuously appreciating currency will cause wage bargaining parties to reflect on the reason for this development, and eventually they will demand abandonment of the incomes policy, because there is no reason why prices below international levels and wages below the value of the marginal product should enable foreigners to incur a welfare gain. In addition, and independent of the exchange rate regime, the question arises: if wages and prices are subject to an incomes policy, should interest income be exempt? Proponents of the 'market anti-inflation plan' and tax-based incomes policy, developed during the past two decades, may claim that their proposals are not subject to these limitations. However, theoretical analysis, reviewed in the following section, did not succeed in proving the validity of these concepts.

3. Market-based incomes policy

Theoretical analysis has established two types of incomes policy that use economic incentives to discourage wage and price increases and are thus market-based. Tax-based incomes policy relies on taxing wage or price increases. Market incentive plans are based on the idea that if inflation constitutes the case of an adverse externality, then the theory of property rights is applicable and hence these externalities could be internalized through issuance of rights (freely tradable, perhaps in the form of certificates) to raise wages and/or prices. Given that the five considered Eastern European countries adopted incomes policies relying on taxation of wages, a review of their theoretical analysis appears appropriate, and is given below. First, with regard to 'market anti-inflation plans' (MAP), the following remarks may be made.

a. Market anti-inflation plan

Market anti-inflation plans were pioneered by Lerner (1978), Colander (1979), Lerner and Colander (1980), who proposed to establish a market to set the price of raising price. As mentioned above, the basic premise is that markets are monopolized and therefore unemployment is higher than it would have to be. Specifically, under the assumption of excess supply equilibrium, due to more monopolization on the part of sellers than on the part of buyers, the non-inflationary unemployment rate is above the 'natural' rate. The aim is to raise the costs of monopolization. An economic entity wishing to raise a price or wage has to acquire the right permitting him to do so. In theory, the overall price level remains constant with individual prices flexible. A perceived nonfunctional aspect of price increases (inefficient rent) would be eliminated, the functional aspect would remain.

The questions raised by MAP may be summarized as follows: first, the proponents acknowledge significant administrative difficulties. Second, even if product markets are dominantly monopolistic or oligopolistic, it is not clear to what extent profit margins include inefficient rent. These positions may have been achieved owing to innovative entrepreneurship and could be temporary. The latter should, to the extent possible, be guaranteed by anti-trust laws (including patent regulation) securing openness of markets. The concept of 'workable competition' suggests that under oligopolistic conditions competition may be more intense than in an ideal world of perfect competition. An example could be the following: industries with large profit margins tend to have a large share of total costs accounted for by research activities, suggesting research to be a positive function of profits. It is rent-seeking which contributes to economic growth (although at the same time hindering growth if it succeeds in limiting competition). Hence many of the profit margins suspected by incomes policy advocates as being inefficient could be remuneration for research and risk-taking entrepreneurship in the broadest sense. If these rents are curtailed, the consequence would be less entrepreneurship, less growth and less employment. Third, conflicts may arise if base money growth (due, for instance, to financing of fiscal deficits) increases the price of the rights to raise price to a very high level or if, during a given period, this growth exceeds the amount of price increases permitted by rights outstanding. Fourth, price and wage setters could be less inclined to change prices which would adversely affect resource allocation. Fifth, the regulation of price setting by newcomers could be a problem.

Sixth, if market-based incomes policy is a substitute for both a perceived lack of competition on product and labour markets, the question arises as to why incomes policy is superior to policies attempting to secure competition. In sum, MAP proposals may underestimate the importance of profit margins or view them pessimistically, underestimate the importance of policies securing competition, and shift responsibility from authorities who control the fiscal balance and base money growth to those who have to cope with the consequences of expansionary policies.

In light of these difficulties, it is not surprising for the theoretical analysis of incomes policy during the past two decades to be inconclusive. Regarding incomes policy in form of price and value-added incentive schemes, Baumol (1979) and Okun (1981) find for a perfectly competitive industry that a price TIP would reduce output. Koford and Miller (1985) provide a comparative analysis of the Lerner and Colander (1980) proposal of a value-added incentive scheme using Benassy's (1982) disequilibrium framework. They show that by increasing the marginal revenue of lowering the product price and decreasing the marginal revenue of raising the price, a MAP results in the firm's perceived demand curve to be more elastic. This could be interpreted as a confirmation of the stated welfare gains of MAP incomes policy. However, the authors' model is static which is precisely the underlying problem of MAP proposals (economic interpretation of profit margins) and the authors also find that the dampening impact on inflation and unemployment tends to decline with a rise of the target real wage trade unions seek. Departing from the theoretical work in terms of macroeconomic models, one fundamental problem of MAP proposals appears to be their assessment of inflation as an externality caused by private market participants.

b. Tax-based incomes policy

The earliest proposal of a market-based incomes policy was conceived in recognition of the fact that in an economy where price and wage determination is decentralized, an incomes policy in the form of moral suasion will lack effectiveness. The Wallich-Weintraub (1971) tax-based incomes policy proposed levying a surcharge on the corporate profits tax for firms granting wage increases in excess of a norm.[20] Use of the profits tax was suggested to prevent a shift of the tax to buyers. The proposal was presented without an underlying theory, which was later provided by Lerner and Colander (1980). However, substantiating one of two basic premises of the proposal and providing a theoretical argument, Weintraub (1972) interpreted inflation during the post war period as being of the 'cost-push' type, suggesting non-demand phenomena, as monopolistic and administered prices, to be the primary cause for inflation. While not universally accepted, the distinction between 'cost-push'- and 'demand-pull' inflation may justify use of taxes in the cost-push case, whereas the latter would require demand management. The second premise of the proposal is that

14

employers resist wage demands so that a new, significant source of tax revenue is not created. Subsequently, a variety of tax-based schemes were conceived, several of them aiming at increasing compliance, notably a proposal which was adopted by the United States Carter administration in 1978.[21] Canterbery's (1983) proposal to levy a tax on value-added growth in excess of a firm's growth of output and factor productivity is noteworthy, because it does not discriminate between different sources of income. To keep distortions created by a wage tax at a minimum, avoid both the above mentioned fiscal problem and discouraging productivity bargains, and raise the feasible real wage without causing an equal change in the target real wage, Jackman and Layard (1990) suggest a tax on average hourly wages at the firm level, which can be negative due to payment of a fixed per worker subsidy. In addition to the narrowing of the gap between target and feasible real wage, the consideration of a subsidy may reduce harm to allocative efficiency, because a penalty-only TIP could induce not only substitution of labour for capital but also debt for equity. With a penalty-reward TIP the latter substitution effect could be eliminated (Seidman, 1978). Using a one- and two sector real model they show how this increasing wedge between labour costs and earnings results in a lower target real wage and NAIRU, and hence in a higher employment level. However, there are considerable doubts about the allocative and social welfare aspects of TIP:[22] provided the tax does not cover all sectors, which, for political reasons, appears likely, resources may be shifted; tax avoidance through use of non-price methods is likely to occur; with a rise in the tax rate, the variance around the average wage decreases, hence impeding the allocative function of relative wage changes; the tradeoff between skilled and non-skilled labour is distorted (hiring expensive labour is discouraged); the policy may lead to net revenues or, in the case of a simultaneously granted subsidy, possibly net expenditures, raising the question as to their distortions; there is the question as to the incidence: if firms view the tax as an increase in marginal costs, it will be passed on to prices and, in the case of mark-up pricing, the shifting will be total; most importantly, a tax-based incomes policy may reduce investment incentives, because it can be considered an indirect tax on investment which would imply favoring of declining industries at the expense of growing ones (Moene, 1990). Hence, the tax may be detrimental to long run growth. Regarding the income distribution, the tax will not cause changes as long as a decline in wage inflation is matched by a decline in the price level. Under mark-up pricing, this would require no effect on the mark-up. However, if the tax would cause a decline in investment, growth of both the marginal efficiency of labour and capital would, *ceteris paribus*, likely differ with a resulting impact on the income distribution.

Given very limited empirical evidence on tax-based incomes policy,[23] Diamond (1990) suggests to study the evolution of unemployment in the United States during times when payroll taxes rose which were used to finance increases in planned retirement benefits. With the retirement benefit formula being progressive, such a payroll tax increase may be seen as an approximation of taxing earnings and returning the revenue as a lump sum. Although such an examination is obviously insufficient, apparently there have been no noticeable effects on unemployment. It may be concluded the theoretical analysis regarding allocative and social welfare aspects of tax-based incomes policy is inconclusive. Empirical evidence on tax-based incomes policy is insufficient.

Notes

1   As of January 1993 the Czech and Slovak Federal Republic was divided into the independent Czech and Slovak Republics. Since the data used in this study cover the period until end of 1992, the republics are treated as one country.

2   It is not controversial that inflation, above a certain very moderate level, decreases welfare, owing to distributional effects and distortions of resource allocation. While allocational distortions imply a loss of output, the loss will not, however, necessarily be substantial, even at very high levels of inflation. A precondition for this is for the price mechanism to remain unhindered. During the German hyperinflation in the 1920s there were no wage and price controls and real output did not fall until the end of that period. By contrast, the hyperinflation following the end of second World War, attempted to be suppressed by price controls, entailed an output decline of about one half. Inflation at a very moderate level may, however, be socially optimal, for two reasons: first, in contrast to most other taxes, inflation does not entail collection costs. (Thus, using the inflation tax necessitates to consider a trade off between reduction of collection costs, on the one hand, and increases in distortions and income redistributional effects, on the other). Second, optimal taxation theory suggests to tax only final goods (goods that are included in utility functions) so as to remain on the production possibility frontier. Hence, the general assumption of money being an intermediate and not a final good suggests not to apply the inflation tax. However, as shown in Guidotti and Vegh (1991), considering money to be an intermediate good does not necessarily imply that it should not be taxed.

3   Although not discussed theoretically, Haberler (1971 and 1982) emphasized this distinction.

4   Usage of the term 'incomes policy' for all of these measures may not facilitate analysis, because it could create confusion. These measures are policies directed to improve the functioning of the price mechanism. In this paper usage of the term 'incomes policy' is confined to measures that aim directly at restraining growth of the aggregate wage level, such as moral suasion policy to influence growth of wages, taxes on wage increases, wage growth guidelines, and wage controls.

5   Given general agreement that influencing the allocational and distributional results obtained in this type of market economy through indirect means enhances individual freedom, the term 'total' market economy may be more appropriate than 'free' market economy.

6   It may be noted, first, that the problems posed by externalities, unstable market equilibria or equilibria that are judged to require too much time until attainable cannot be held against the view that the price mechanism is capable to achieving total plan coordination, because they may largely be avoided on account of the mentioned policies available to secure proper functioning of the price mechanism. The problem of the public good cannot be taken as evidence of failure of the price mechanism either, because a public good is not marketable. Second, one school of thought, social-neoliberalism (represented, for instance, by von Hayek (1948), Eucken (1952)) concentrated on defining an institutional order that would secure the price mechanism's proper functioning so as to make a market economy stable in the long run. There have been few instances in history when economic policy followed closely the ideas of an economic school of thought. Social-neoliberalism may claim that its policy recommendations were implemented in rather pure form and thus empirically tested, namely during the period of about 1958 until 1966 in the Federal Republic of Germany. Among other principles, economic policies followed (with some exceptions), the rules of no interference with the price mechanism, open borders for trade, creation of an institutional framework that sought, in particular, to securing a high degree of competition (elimination of distributional conflict) and provision of a social safety net of moderate form. The period witnessed high, non-inflationary growth and it may be argued that unsustainable developments of the mentioned forms did not occur. Subsequently, it may appear that successful rent-seeking resulted in government regulations protecting interests of particular groups. The shares in GDP of the public sector, public consumption, public debt, taxes, subsidies, and social security contributions rose, adversely affecting the price mechanism's functioning through distorted relative prices and by hindering both mobility of factors of production and competition. Incentives to work, save and invest were weakened. When the economy had to cope with large adverse real shocks in the 1970s, these inflexibilities contributed to the experience of relatively high unemployment since then.

7   As already noted, besides determination of resource allocation and income distribution, plan coordination through the price mechanism meets objectives commonly held important on ethical grounds such as individual freedom. There is no coercion to achieve plan coordination.

8   Natural monopolies are an exception.

9   Given the distortions present in world trade, liberalized trade would not be a first best solution. However, to find an optimal tariff structure corre-

17

sponding to these permanently changing distortions is excluded. It may be argued that if a group of countries, burdened by severe adjustment, permits open borders for trade, this would constitute a case for other countries and regional trade agreements to provide for lower trade barriers and, hence, possibly reduced distortions. In addition, low trade barriers counteract highly concentrated markets. It may be mentioned that had the proposals to introduce a temporary across the board tariff in Eastern European countries been followed (meant to mitigate depreciation of the capital stock due to adverse supply and demand shocks and thus meant to protect production and employment), future costs would have arisen: the higher the tariff, the larger would be the depreciation of the then relatively young capital stock occurring at the time the tariff would be lifted. Tariffs played a very limited role in centrally planned economies and most of the tariffs maintained by the five Eastern European countries covered by this study (the tariff structures are rather similar) are presently at the moderate 5-15 per cent level with the lowest tariffs, on average, levied on raw materials and capital goods and the highest tariffs, on average, levied on consumer goods and particularly agricultural goods.

10 Examples of the large body of literature on stabilization are Tobin (1980), Williamson (1985), Bruno (1986), Dornbusch and Simonsen (1987). When inertia is present, the inflationary process could be approximated by a random walk, possibly with drift, given by:

$$p = \alpha + p_{t-1} + v$$

where p is the inflation rate, α is drift and v denotes supply and demand shocks. However, since there are ways to decompose shocks, it would appear preferable to include proxies for them when running such a regression so as to avoid the coefficient of lagged inflation capturing shifts in demand and supply which would cause one to falsely find evidence of inertial inflation when, in fact, there is none. This point has first been made clear by Sachs (1983). VAR analysis can be utilized for shock decomposition (see Blanchard and Quah (1989)).

11 If an individual complies with a disinflationary guideline, he or she will suffer a decline in the real wage or profit, whereas those who do not comply, benefit from a lower price level (free-rider problem). Everyone could be better off if wage and price restraint was obeyed (provided relative wages and prices would not be affected so that distortions are not created) and thus inflation reduced. However, the individual does not know whether others will comply and therefore faces a dilemma (standard prisoner's dilemma). Lipnowski and Maital (1985) and Bull and Schotter (1985) are examples of game theoretic models of incomes policy. Some authors, however, criticize the traditional prisoner's dilemma analysis for failing to

18

acknowledge that the root cause of inflation is the income distribution conflict. For instance, Rakowski (1983, p. 600) suggests that incomes policy may never succeed in achieving a stable equilibrium with low inflation, because the resulting income distribution is likely to be universally condemned as unfair.

12 Experiences with controls applied to break inflationary hysteresis are examined, for instance, in Dornbusch and Simonsen (1987). Two points may be mentioned: if inflation is very high, successful stabilization may be expected to immediately improve the fiscal balance, because lower inflation will raise both real tax revenues (Tanzi effect) and real money demand (higher revenues from seignorage). This could corroborate the case for temporary incomes policy and even imposition of controls. On the other hand, if adjustment is required when inflation is relatively moderate, consistently implemented restrictive policies may suffice to achieve an immediate positive impact on growth, because consistency determines expectations. The crucial role of expectations with respect to the sign of the immediate impact is demonstrated in Giavazzi and Pagano (1990).

13 See, for instance, Layard (1986) and Alogoskoufis and Manning (1988).

14 To mention only very few proponents of incomes policy, see Galbraith (1952), Colander (1985), Layard (1982, 1986, 1990, 1991), Tobin (1987a, b), Alogoskoufis and Manning (1988).

15 In Layard's view, even a situation characterized by approximate equality of job vacancies and unemployment could provide a case for incomes policy (Layard, 1982, p. 220). It may appear difficult to follow this argument, because the question arises as to how wage growth above the feasible growth rate could be prevented if incomes policy would succeed in reducing unemployment below vacancies.

16 Unemployment is affected by the unemployment benefit system put in place. There is evidence supporting the hypothesis for long-term unemployment to be positively related to both the length of unemployment benefit availability and the replacement ratio (ratio of benefit income to income in work), see, for instance, Blanchard et. al. (1989) and Layard (1990). However, measures are available to increase incentives to seek work without curtailing unemployment benefits.

17 For Western European countries Layard (1990) finds the contribution of wage-bargaining arrangements to the variation of unemployment to be about equal to policies toward the unemployed (duration of unemployment compensation, replacement ratio, training programs etc.). The relation between organization of wage bargaining and unemployment is discussed in Section 3.

18 In a number of countries, particularly in Austria and Sweden, wage negotiating parties appear to have found the fixed exchange rate system credible and to have accounted for it in bargaining. Prior to bargaining governments emphasized adherence to the adopted exchange rate target.

19

19 Assuming mark-up pricing and using log form, a price equation in an open economy may be written:

$$p = w - x + m + p_m$$

where p denotes the overall inflation rate, w is the rate of growth of the aggregate wage level, x is the growth rate of aggregate labour productivity, m is the growth rate of the aggregate profit mark-up, and p_m is the growth rate of the import price level converted to domestic currency. The equation shows that in an open economy a rise of the aggregate nominal wage level in line with aggregate productivity is neither a necessary nor sufficient condition for the price level to remain stable. However, at least in the long run, p tends to move in line with growth of base money. This may raise the question whether the adverse externality society bears due to 'creeping' inflation, which is supposed to rationalize government interference in the market process by an incomes policy, is related to the responsibility of the institution who has control over base money growth.

20 The corporate profits tax rate t for the ith firm, including the excess wage tax, is given by:

$$t_i = b + \alpha (\Delta w_i - n)$$

where b is the base tax rate, α is the policy determined wage tax multiplier ($\alpha > 0$), Δw_i is the average percentage wage increase of firm i, and n is the wage norm.

21 The proposal included a 'real wage-insurance' scheme so as to avoid the free-rider and prisoners' dilemma inherent in wage guidelines relying on voluntary compliance. The tax rate faced by each individual eligible for the 'insurance' was specified to be:

$$t = b - (\Delta p - z) \text{ for } z < \Delta p \leq 10 \text{ per cent}$$

where b is the tax base on labour income, Δp is the actual rate of change of consumer prices, and z is the threshold rate of price increase which triggers a tax reimbursement. However, the scheme suffers from adverse selection: everyone whose wage increase meets the guidepost, qualifies for the tax credit, even if the norm would have been met in the absence of the scheme and if the difference between the actual inflation rate and the threshold rate was caused by other factors than wage inflation (as, for instance, price increases in primary inputs). Therefore, the proposal was not implemented for Congressional fears of further increases of the fiscal deficit.

22 See, in particular, the analysis in Seidman (1978), Pencavel (1981), and Paci (1988) provide discussions.

23 Hungary's policy of wage control, employed during 1968 until a TIP was introduced in 1988, resembles a TIP. France employed a value-added TIP during 1974 until 1977. For nine months in 1976, Belgium also implemented a variant. However, these experiences do not provide insights, since the Hungarian economy was centrally planned, coverage of the French tax was limited, and the Belgian episode was too short. Regarding the Belgian case it should be mentioned, however, that wage growth was successfully dampened with the excess tax revenue having been marginal. The Hungarian experience is described in Csikos-Nagy (1989), for details on the French and Belgian experience see Chand (1986).

3 Incomes policy in international perspective

Turning to the experiences industrial countries had with incomes policies during the past three decades, in the *United States* there have been four attempts to control upward movement of prices and wages.[1] The primary reasons to implement these policies were demand effects resulting from both war experiences and expansionary policies. Paradoxically, rapid price increases following the second period of incomes policy, when union vs. non-union wage differentials were restored to their pre-incomes period level, and following the third period, when profit margins were restored, appear to have contributed to subsequent pursuance of incomes policy (Pencavel, 1981). The first attempt was a policy of wage and price controls, lasting from September 1950 to February 1953 (Korean war). The controls were abandoned due to various Congressional measures weakening the effectiveness of price controls, and a presidential intervention (in late 1952) sanctioning a negotiated wage increase in excess of that approved by a Wage Stabilization Board. From 1962 to 1966 a policy of wage-price guideposts was in place, adopted as a response to expansionary monetary policy and the believe (expressed in the Economic Report of the President in January 1962) that a considerable non-competitive sector existed whose discretionary powers of price and wage determination could be curbed if a guidelines policy provided for a sensitive public opinion.[2] As in 1953, the government abandoned the policy shortly after the president sanctioned a wage increase in excess of the wage guidepost. In response to accelerating inflation and the recession in 1970, the Economic Stabilization Act of 1970 (effective for four years) granted the president the power to impose a temporary wage-price freeze. A ninety-day freeze on all wages, prices, and profits was declared which was supposed to be a longer-term programme of controls to reduce inflation. Following the first oil price shock in 1973, and the concomitant large changes in relative prices, no attempt was made to continue the controls when the Economic Stabilization Act expired in early 1974. In response to a switch to expansionary monetary and fiscal policy in 1977 with subsequent accelerating inflation, a fourth attempt to pursue an incomes policy was undertaken from end 1978 to 1979. The programme provided for price and wage controls in form of guidelines without imposing non-compliance costs.[3] As a result, the pay and price standards were adjusted several times to accommodate collective bargaining agreements. In 1979 union labour was promised an important role in determining new wage guidelines, thus weakening the policy. An attempt to avoid the 'free rider' problem through introduction of the above described variant of tax-based incomes policy, the 'real wage insurance' scheme, failed.

Regarding econometric analysis of the impact of incomes policy on inflation in general, the greatest difficulty is given by the unknown noncontrol state. Apart from this problem, ideally, a simultaneous model of wage and price determination would be needed, which would explicitly consider price expectations formation. As regards the latter, specification of non-myopic expectations advanced considerably (Henry and Omerod, 1979, Sargan, 1980, Wallis, 1980). However, their application in standard wage and price determination models did not significantly alter or improve results. Competing explanations of inflation are reflected in the large number of estimated models. Commonly, however, the effects of controls and incomes policy on inflation are estimated using a single price or wage equation that incorporates a dummy variable representing the incomes policy. Hence, these approaches suffer from simultaneous-equations bias, and a potential misinterpretation of the dummy variable coefficient if fiscal and monetary policy are carried out differently during an incomes policy period than they would have been pursued in the absence of it. The dummy variable may not be exogenous.[4] Bearing in mind these limitations of most of the empirical work presented on incomes policies, the major studies regarding the United States (Gordon, 1975, McGuire, 1976, Blinder and Newton, 1979, Pencavel, 1981) agree that the second and third period of incomes policy reduced the rate of price inflation during those periods, and that subsequently inflation was briefly higher than it would have been in the absence of the policy. The results differ significantly with regard to the estimated magnitude of these effects. Pencavel's (1981) results, based on a standard, augmented 'Phillips' curve wage equation,[5] imply that, on average, the controls or incomes policies reduced the rate of change of wages by 0.225 percentage points per quarter. However, none of the obtained negative signs for the dummy variables were statistically significant, a result that held also if, on account of parameter instability, wage change equations were estimated for the different sub-periods. Hence, there is no empirical prove of any appreciable impact of incomes policies pursued in the United States on inflation. Unfortunately, there have been no studies attempting to measure the potential adverse real output effects of controls or incomes policies.

Regarding *European countries*, it is commonly held that Austria, Germany, the Netherlands, and Scandinavian countries pursued permanent incomes policies.[6]

However, controls programs and the measures they adopted to directly influence wage formation have been transitory. Hence, under the definition applied here they pursued either none or transitory incomes policy. Nevertheless, these countries established institutions mitigating distributional conflict. With Eichner (1983), these measures, most of which were undertaken shortly after second world war, may be subsumed under 'planning-subordinated policy,' where the task of balancing income claims is subordinated to some long run planning process so as to maintain the economy's competitive position. This planning process may not be explicit; institutions that internalize distributional conflict may be seen as an equivalent to it. Specifically, Austria, commonly pointed out as an example of successful permanent incomes policy, has a Parity Commission, staffed with few participants (increasing its effectiveness), which absorbs and internalizes distributional conflict. There has been strong centralization of powers within the interest organizations, general agreement that the existing wage structure and functional income distribution are appropriate and that income gains should be received through economic growth (social partnership). The legislative process is viewed to be the appropriate forum regarding changes in income distribution. Wage drift was minor and its skill structure reinforced the negotiated wage structure. Hence, it is the institutional environment and not incomes policy that explains relatively low unemployment. Germany did also not pursue incomes policy.[7] The Netherlands have both a rather decentralized system of wage bargaining with the central employers' federation being rather weak. Perhaps for these reasons there have been several periods of incomes policy, a part of which were frequent government intervention in wage negotiations. Incomes policy consisted largely of tax concessions to wage earners, increased transfers to inactive persons and subsidies to firms. Incomes policies are widely evaluated as ineffective and may have promoted decentralization of bargaining due to restraints to which they subjected trade unions. Contrary to common assertion, wage bargaining systems in Nordic countries (whose unemployment rates, except Denmark, are traditionally low) are not homogeneous. Denmark, and Norway have rather fragmented structures of trade unions and employers' federations and perhaps therefore installed a mediation system with far-reaching powers supplemented by frequent government intervention. Denmark differs from other Nordic countries in that political power tended to be somewhat less stable which could contribute to an explanation of unemployment in so far as it may have inhibited dialogue between the government and trade unions and therefore expectations of trade unions may have been somewhat less stable. Finland has a centralized organizational structure but it had strong communist trade unions causing frequent state intervention. Sweden has more centralized unions and employers' federations and very little government intervention. There are, however, two common features of Scandinavian wage bargaining systems: wage agreements are influenced by macro-model simulations (refinements of Aukrust's (1970) tradeables-non-tradeables model) employed by Expert Committees (Norway, Finland) or labour organizations (Sweden) resulting in joint economic analysis and they all have National Mediators endowed with strong power (Sweden employs an ad-hoc mediation system). Thus, in Scandinavian countries, low unemployment may be largely explained with the institutional environment rather than with incomes policy as defined here. It may be noted that the pursued policy of wage compression in these countries resulted in substantial wage drift, which, in the Norwegian case, was shown to have resulted in contractual wage increases (Addison, 1981), suggesting this policy to have spurred overall wage growth.

Turning to the remaining European countries, Switzerland has not pursued incomes policy.[8] By contrast, the countries with relatively high unemployment Belgium, France, Ireland, Italy, and the United Kingdom have industry level wage bargaining systems with employers' federations commonly ill-coordinated and they all pursued incomes policies under the narrow definition adopted here. These countries permitted indexation of wages (abolished in Italy in 1992) so as to free wage bargaining from inflationary expectations. However, indexation hindered adjustment of the real wage level, required after the oil price shocks in the 1970s, and contributed to 'cost-push' inflation. Given that trade unions added the resulting 'fiscal drag' effect to wage demands, the countries adopted incomes policies of many forms, mainly those espoused by the Netherlands. France had several periods of controls and a transitory VATIP. Incomes policy in the United Kingdom included controls, government intervention in wage bargaining, public sector 'pay increase pauses,' wage compression, and tax concessions. It was abandoned in 1979.

Japan did not pursue incomes policy. Wage bargaining is at the industry level but it is preceded by intensive coordination among employers and unions with settlement in one industry broadly followed elsewhere. The system may be comparable to the one employed in Switzerland (Layard, 1990). Labour-management relations are superior with strikes being short (Aoki, 1988). Wage bargaining systems in *Australia* and *New Zealand* are sui generis, due to the involvement of courts. Both countries pursued incomes policy under the narrow definition adopted here, since measures to directly influence wage formation were taken in the form of permitted wage indexation (following the first oil price shock) and a 'Prices and Incomes Accord' (Australia) under government coordination.

With the exception of French and British policies, econometric analysis of incomes policy in European countries has been relatively limited, which is not surprising, given that controls were the exception rendering appropriate specification of the wage and price equation difficult. The finding that those countries who pursued egalitarian incomes policy did experience high wage drift and possibly accelerated wage growth was already noted. It was also noted that the episodes of TIPs in France and Belgium do not allow meaningful econometric analysis. Analysis of France's incomes policy (summarized in Malinvaud, 1990) yielded that it had a larger impact on wage formation than on the overall price level. The influence of controls is significant and correctly signed. As may have been expected, the price and wage freeze in 1982 appears to have been offset by price rises following the end of controls end of 1983. The legal minimum wage is a significant and correctly signed explanatory variable in the wage equation and correlated with public sector salaries, suggesting that it contributes to overall wage growth. Regarding the United Kingdom, Whitley, 1986 used the above mentioned simultaneous three equations model, where the incomes policy variable is endogenized and adjusted for its presumed effectiveness (incomes policy being defined in the common broad sense). He finds this variable to have a highly significant, correctly signed impact on wage and price inflation. Nevertheless, such findings may not be read as proof for incomes policy to improve alignment of wage growth with productivity growth: the periods of restraint were usually followed by periods of accelerated wage growth so that it is not clear whether long run behaviour was influenced; one theoretical consequence of successful restraint through incomes policy could have been deteriorating labour-management relations resulting in more strikes and many more questions along these lines arise.

Regarding Australia, Lewis and Kirby (1988) depart from concentrating on the 'Phillips' curve approach and use a simple model of supply of and demand for labour with the impact of incomes policy attempted to be captured by a dummy variable included in both equations. They find the period of wage indexation (1975-81) and the period of 'Prices and Incomes Accord' (1982-87) to have resulted not in a shift of labour demand but in a downward shift of labour supply: during the former period equilibrium real wages were about 3 per cent lower and during the latter period about 10 per cent lower, than without incomes policy. In their view, this raised equilibrium employment by about 3 per cent and 8 per cent, respectively. Further findings are: the second period of incomes policy increased somewhat the adjustment speed of employment, real unemployment benefits appear to negatively influence labour supply, and adjustment of employment to labour market shocks appears to be relatively slow. While these results could lend support to the forms of incomes policy Australia adopted, such an interpretation is subject to qualifications: the major problem is that it is not known whether in the long run unemployment would be lower and economic growth higher without incomes policy but competitiveness of the economy maintained through restricted base money growth, lower fiscal deficits, lower trade barriers, open markets, increased incentives for unemployed to search work, and consequently lower inflationary expectations. The latter may have caused the adoption of incomes policy in the first place. These policies could also be expected to improve the estimated relatively slow speed of adjustment of the labour market.

It may thus be concluded that implemented incomes policies in industrial countries show a common thread: they appear to have been a political necessity but they were adopted often in forms incompatible with a market economy and without knowing what their consequences are and there is no evidence that these policies had a positive impact on long run growth and employment. The effect of incomes policy on inflation appears to have been temporary. Regarding the United States an equilibrium may have been disturbed and restored following the abandonment of the policy so that gains in welfare are unlikely. In several cases in Western Europe, incomes policy appears to have promoted itself: first, wage indexation to the consumer price level was permitted inhibiting adjustment of real wages to adverse external shocks and resulting in accelerated inflation and 'fiscal drag,' then tax concessions were granted to offset this latter impact on real household income and profit, causing fiscal balances to deteriorate, because expenditure growth had become accustomed to the 'fiscal drag' effect. The deteriorating fiscal balances, in turn, resulted in further incomes policy measures in an attempt to promote growth. Before evaluating incomes policies adopted by Eastern European countries, the following section reviews the developments that resulted in their adoption.

Notes

1   Braun (1986) and Pencavel (1981) provide chronologies.
2   The guideposts were designed such that wage increases were related to changes in labour productivity while price changes had to reflect changes in costs. They were (ineffectively) monitored by the Council of Economic Advisors. There were no official penalties for non-compliance.
3   Assuming a simple firm's maximizing profit function, the probability of non-compliance increases, *ceteris paribus*, first, the smaller the probability of being detected by incomes policy control agents, second, the greater the gap between the controlled and uncontrolled price, and third, the smaller the fine imposed for non-compliance. In addition, it is intuitively clear that non-compliance is the more likely, the larger the absolute value of the price elasticity of demand with regard to the own price or own wage (for a formal prove see Pencavel (1981, p. 179)). This outcome remains unchanged if a firm maximizes revenue per worker (labour managed firm).
4   This problem of omitted feedback from the level of inflation to the strength of incomes policy (which results in the coefficient of the incomes policy variable to be biased towards zero) caused Whitley (1986) to suggest the use of quantitative indicators in the form of an index of policy. Real wage pressure of policy is adjusted for policy intensity in terms of government 'toughness' and trade union cooperation. Although his simultaneous model of a wage and price equation and policy reaction function is partial, it shows how incomes policy can be endogenized.

27

5   The equation was of the form:

$$\Delta W_t = \alpha_0 + \alpha_1 U_{t-1}^{-1} + \alpha_2 \Delta x_{t-1} + \alpha_3 \Delta p_{t-1} + \alpha_4 I_t$$
$$+ \alpha_5 (U_{t-1}^{-1} I_t) + \alpha_6 (\Delta x_{t-1} I_t) + \alpha_7 (\Delta p_{t-1} I_t) + v_t$$

where Δw_t denotes the rate of change of average hourly wage, U_{t-1}^{-1} denotes the inverse of the unemployment rate in the previous quarter, Δx_{t-1} is the annual rate of change of industrial production, Δp_{t-1} is the annual rate of change of the index of industrial production, and I_t is the dummy variable taking the value unity when an incomes policy is in effect and zero otherwise. The equation was estimated using quarterly data. A survey of wage equations ranging from nominal wage and earnings models to real wage models of the error correction type can be found in Henry (1981).

6   Incomes policies in European countries are analyzed in Addison (1981), Flanagan et. al. (1983), Braun (1986), Urquidi (1989), Elvander (1990).

7   Government interventions in wage bargaining did not occur, but an institutional environment was implemented reducing conflict. Wage bargaining is centralized. Despite these features and relatively stable political power, unemployment since the 1970s has been relatively high, generally explained with structural rigidities stemming from unemployment benefits with a high replacement ratio and long duration resulting, in turn, in an insider-outsider problem and little incentive to search work.

8   Bargaining is decentralized, but employers' federations are well coordinated and relatively strong, a law requires 'peace agreements' hindering strikes, and there is, similar to Austria, considerable political consensus. Hence, the institutional set up contributes to low unemployment.

4 Macro and microeconomic developments since 1990 and implemented incomes policies

1. Macroeconomic developments

Following the political changes in 1989, the initial conditions for implementation of macroeconomic adjustment and structural reform programs were not similar in the five Eastern European countries. Specifically, the Czech and Slovak Federal Republic and Hungary had, to their advantage, pursued rather conservative economic policies as a result of which there were no major macroeconomic imbalances: neither had there been substantial repressed inflation (despite controls of more than 80 per cent and 40 per cent of consumer prices, respectively), posing the problem of eliminating a monetary overhang, nor had there been a pressing external debt servicing problem. By contrast, Bulgaria, Poland and Romania faced a situation of large excess demand at the then prevailing price levels and were burdened by relatively large external debt servicing payments. Romania had nearly entirely repaid its external debt by the end of 1989, but this had been achieved on cost of growth during the previous decade concomitant with a substantial deterioration of the physical capital stock due to forgone investment. However, given that the economies of all five countries were largely centrally planned with very limited private ownership of means of production, the structure of input and consumer prices was distorted through price regulations, subsidies, and overvalued currencies, and the institutional framework was not capable of supporting private economic activity. Hence, as shown in Appendix I, at the outset, the adopted reform strategies were nearly identical with differences occurring only with regard to the preferred exchange rate system and the approach and speed chosen in implementing privatization and institutional reform.[1] While microeconomic reforms of a transformation to a market economy entail a loss of output,[2] by the end of 1990, the five economies suffered additional adverse demand shocks, due to the loss of their traditional export market, the former Soviet Union, and markets in the Middle

Table 4.1
Selected Eastern European countries:
terms of trade indices [a]

(1985 = 100)

	1989	1990	1991
(Rounded)			
Bulgaria	—	—	—
Czech and Slovak Federal Republic	112	109	93
Hungary	102	101	92
Poland	127	111	97
Romania [b]	122	83	88

Source: International Monetary Fund, Data Fund.

a Defined as export price index divided by import price index.
b Terms of trade proxied by inverse of real effective exchange rate; (1980 = 100).

East, and they faced an adverse supply shock in the form of increased import prices (to international levels), particularly for petroleum, raw materials and intermediate inputs.[3] Hungary's economy was hit by an additional supply shock due to a severe drought. The impact on output due to these demand and supply shocks, exacerbated by spill-over effects among the five countries, broadly corresponded to the degree of openness of the five economies (Table 4.2):[4] Figure 4.1 shows that Bulgaria, with the highest degree of openness, endured the largest output decline, followed by Romania who had the second largest degree of openness. Despite being a significantly less open economy than Hungary, Poland suffered a somewhat larger output decline which may be attributable, to a large extent, to the fact that Hungary, in contrast to Poland, had permitted about 50 per cent of consumer prices to be market determined during several

Table 4.2
Selected Eastern European countries: "Openness" *

(As per cent of GDP)

	1989	1990	1991	1992
Bulgaria	112	253	110	98
Czech and Slovak Federal Republic	56	61	73	65
Hungary	67	54	62	63
Poland	32	51	37	36
Romania	80	66	42	57

Source: International Monetary Fund, Data Fund.

* Sum of imports plus exports as per cent of GDP. 1992 figures are estimates.

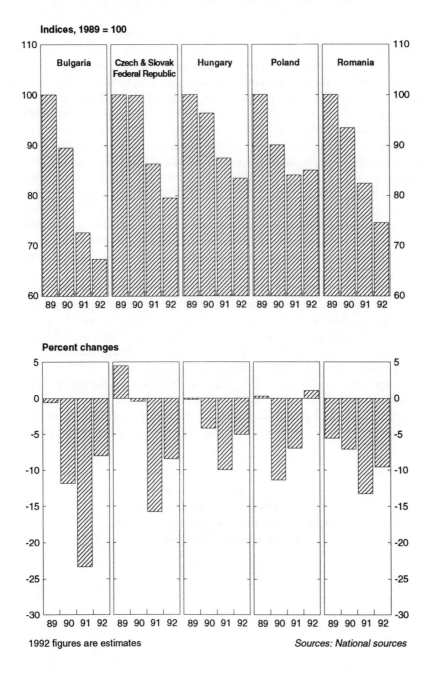

Indices, 1989 = 100

Bulgaria | Czech & Slovak Federal Republic | Hungary | Poland | Romania

Percent changes

1992 figures are estimates   *Sources: National sources*

Figure 4.1   Selected Eastern European countries: real gross domestic
product

31

years prior to transition, and thus resource allocation may have been less distorted in this economy. However, in all five countries, the statistically measured falls in output and the real wage developments discussed below do not permit an inference as to the evolution of living standards: first, under central-planning and dependent on heavy industry's share in output, income appears to have been generated without contributing to a rise in production of consumer goods. Heavy industries within the CMEA region may have been a nearly closed production cycle. Hence, to the extent that production of goods and services is ended which is not part of the division of labour to generate consumer goods, mainly the utility of those is affected who were employed in these activities. Second, having been shortage economies, utility of consumers was lowered due to queuing, bribery, use of substitutes for demanded goods, and black market activity. Therefore, a fall in the real wage can be associated with a rise in utility, because official prices prior to their liberalization were lower than effective prices which incorporate the utility decreasing consequences of shortages (Lipton and Sachs, 1990).

Access to world markets and immediately granted (limited) access to the market of the European Communities (EC) implied, however, a positive supply shock and enabled the Czech and Slovak Federal Republic and Hungary to maintain, and Poland to even increase, the value of total exports (Table 4.3), dampening the recession. For Bulgaria and Romania, with substantially larger shares of exports in GDP prior to transition, and less close ties to Western markets, this switching has been more difficult. Table 4.3a shows that presently virtually all trade is denominated in convertible currencies. Figure 4.1 demonstrates also that in the years during which the major liberalization measures were taken (1990 for Poland and 1991 for the other countries), the output loss

Table 4.3

Selected Eastern European countries:
exports of goods and services in convertible
and non-convertible currencies

(In billions of U.S. dollars)

	1989	1990	1991	1992 *
Bulgaria	8.3	3.8	4.0	4.2
Czech and Slovak Federal Republic	17.1	14.4	13.5	13.0
Hungary	10.4	9.1	9.7	10.6
Poland	13.7	17.4	15.2	16.6
Romania	10.5	5.9	3.9	4.2

Source: International Monetary Fund, Data Fund.

* Estimates.

Table 4.3a
Selected Eastern European countries:
share of exports of goods and services not denominated in convertible currencies in total exports of goods and services

(As per cent)

	1989	1990	1991	1992 *
Bulgaria	61.7	31.3	6.1	1.1
Czech and Slovak Federal Republic	59.5	46.8	19.3	0.8
Hungary	28.5	17.9	0.5	0.3
Poland	36.2	26.5	2.0	1.2
Romania	42.3	42.7	17.3	2.6

Source: International Monetary Fund, Data Fund.

* Estimates.

was largest. The decreasing decline of output during 1992 in all countries may be taken as an indication for the contraction to have bottomed out and for growth to be likely to resume.

Among the first measures taken in reforming their economies, all five countries liberalized a substantial share of consumer and input prices and reduced subsidies.[5] Accordingly, inflation, as measured by the consumer price index (Figure 4.2), rose sharply in the respective years of liberalization and in excess of money supply growth adjusted for decline in output. An exception is Hungary due to the relatively lower share of prices that remained controlled prior to reform. Bulgaria, Poland and Romania experienced relatively large price level increases, in excess of adjusted money supply growth, which may be taken as an indication of comparatively larger pent-up excess demand prior to reform. To some extent, it could, however, also be attributable to monopoly power on the part of major enterprises and/or overshooting prices due to both the experience of excess demand and labour managed firm behaviour. Regarding 1992, the first year after the major one time price adjustment for the countries except Poland, annual consumer price inflation is estimated to have followed roughly adjusted growth of the money supply. An exception is Romania, where the halt of credit expansion proved more difficult resulting in a sharply increasing money supply in 1991.

Figure 4.3 suggests that the absorption approach may be applied to explaining external current account movements. Bulgaria, Poland, and Romania experienced current account deficits when the fiscal balance was negative. The fact that in Hungary and in the former Czech and Slovak Federal Republic fiscal deficits have increased since 1990 concomitant with some improvement of the external current account balances may be explained with substantial increases of savings on the part of private households (Table 4.4). Figure 4.3 shows that during 1990, the first year of transition (with the exception of

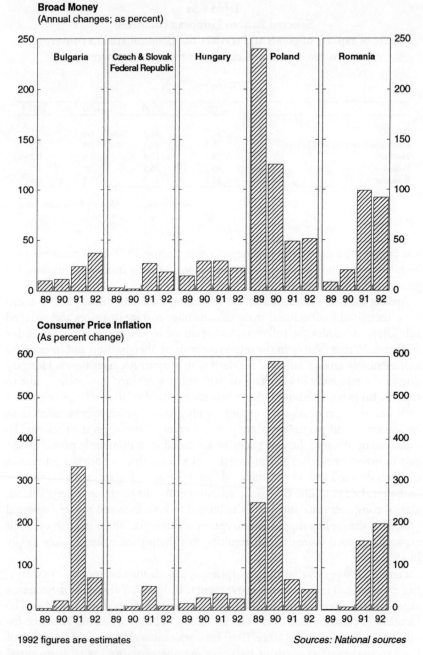

Figure 4.2   Selected Eastern European countries: broad money and
consumer price inflation

Bulgaria, whose transition began in 1991) all countries experienced a substantial improvement of their fiscal balance, mainly on account of beginning reductions in subsidies and taxation of fictitious profits due to historical cost accounting (Schaffer, 1992). In the following year 1991, more substantial reductions of subsidies occurred, but these savings were outweighed by declining tax revenues for three main reasons: tax rates were lowered on income and profit taxes, inflation resulted in losses of real tax revenues due to lags in collection (Tanzi-effect), and social security expenditures rose. Bulgaria did not tax fictitious profits, partly explaining relatively higher fiscal deficits. Although inflation has been reduced in 1992, alleviating the second reason for deteriorating fiscal balances, social security expenditures are estimated to have risen in

Table 4.4
Selected Eastern European countries:
savings ratios of private households

(As per cent)

	1989	1990	1991*
Bulgaria	9.9	8.7	13.4
Czech and Slovak Federal Republic	3.5	0.5	6.1
Hungary	3.3	8.3	12.1
Poland	19.8	19.2	—
Romania	6.0	12.1	6.9

Source: International Monetary Fund, Data Fund.

* Estimates.

Table 4.5
Selected Eastern European countries:
gross fixed capital formation

(As per cent of GDP)

	1989	1990	1991*
Bulgaria	26.4	23.9	8.5
Czech and Slovak Federal Republic	26.5	27.1	21.8
Hungary	25.7	23.0	23.3
Poland	16.4	19.6	17.4
Romania	29.6	20.0	13.1

Source: International Monetary Fund, Data Fund.

* Estimates.

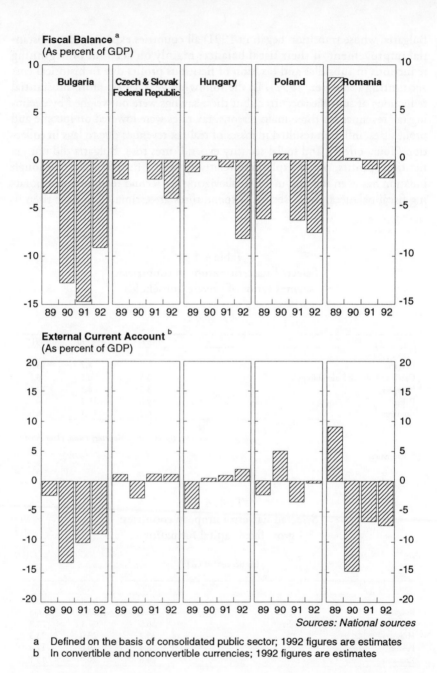

Fiscal Balance [a]
(As percent of GDP)

Bulgaria | Czech & Slovak Federal Republic | Hungary | Poland | Romania

External Current Account [b]
(As percent of GDP)

Sources: National sources

a   Defined on the basis of consolidated public sector; 1992 figures are estimates
b   In convertible and nonconvertible currencies; 1992 figures are estimates

Figure 4.3   Selected Eastern European countries: fiscal balance and external current account

this year despite widespread cuts in unemployment compensations, and tax receipts fell further as a share of GDP in all countries, owing, in part, to reduced profitability of the state enterprise sectors, which, in turn, is attributable, in part, to nominal wage increases.[6] Despite increasing fiscal deficits, investment activity on the part of governments declined (Table 4.5), indicating a structural deterioration of government expenditures.

Figure 4.4 plots the estimated evolution of unemployment, real wages, and productivity. There are reservations as to the adequacy of these data. The margin of error is large, particularly regarding real wages and productivity. Real wage changes in the chart were obtained using the CPI as deflator (real consumption wage). Owing to cuts in consumer good subsidies, the CPIs rose by more than producer price levels. Hence, an unchanged real product wage would have meant a decrease of the real consumption wage. Wage demands to compensate for the cut in subsidies would have left profits unchanged, had taxation of enterprises been lowered and had productivity remained constant. However, productivity declined and taxation increased, necessitating a fall of real product wages in excess of the productivity decline shown in Figure 4.4 for profits to remain constant. Real product wages, however, fell by less than real consumption wages shown in the chart. In Hungary, real consumption wages declined only marginally. Here, the profit squeeze was, however, less pronounced, due to relatively moderate inflation. In the respective year of price liberalization, Bulgaria, the Czech and Slovak Federal Republic and Poland appear to have experienced a fall of the real product wage level in line with the productivity decline. Thereafter adjustment abated. Changes of productivity adjusted real (consumption) wages together with unemployment rates are shown in Table 4.6. Before evaluating the Table, an additional qualification has to be given: no distinction is made between public and private sector developments. If it was correct to assume that productivity in the private sectors rose during 1990 through 1992, then, given the estimated aggregate productivity declines in each country shown in Figure 4.4, it follows that public sectors (including state-enterprises) suffered a larger productivity decline than shown in the chart, particularly with regard to countries whose private sector contributes a significant share of output (Poland, Romania (Table 4.7)). Hence, the estimated changes of adjusted real wages shown in Table 4.6 would be too optimistic regarding public sectors and their enterprises. Accounting for this qualification and the quality of data, Table 4.6 demonstrates that during the period 1990 through 1992 adjusted real consumption wages are estimated to have increased in Bulgaria, Hungary, and Romania and so did unemployment.[7] By contrast, in the Czech and Slovak Federal Republic adjusted real wages fell substantially during this period and unemployment is estimated to have decreased subsequently.[8] The fall of adjusted real wages during 1990 through 1992 in Poland, associated with rising unemployment, may not be inconsistent with an explanation of unemployment mainly with the real wage level, because Poland has the

Table 4.6
Selected Eastern European countries:
unemployment and productivity adjusted real wage *

(as per cent)

	1990	1991	1992
Bulgaria			
Rate of unemployment	—	10.2	15.3
Productivity adjusted real wage	10.0	-19.1	17.9
Czech and Slovak Federal Republic			
Rate of unemployment	1.0	6.6	5.3
Productivity adjusted real wage	—	-17.0	17.4
Hungary			
Rate of unemployment	1.7	7.7	11.6
Productivity adjusted real wage	3.5	11.3	11.8
Poland			
Rate of unemployment	6.3	11.8	13.1
Productivity adjusted real wage	-23.8	6.2	-6.8
Romania			
Rate of unemployment	—	2.9	9.0
Productivity adjusted real wage	17.1	-1.4	-9.1

Source: International Monetary Fund, Data Fund.

* Unemployment rates are percentage shares of labour force and end of period estimates. Adjusted real wages are changes in the aggregate real wage level minus estimated changes in aggregate productivity, both period average estimates.

largest private sector of the studied countries and thus the productivity decline shown in Figure 4.4 could be significantly underestimated if it was correct to assume productivity in the private sector not to have fallen. Hence, productivity adjusted real wages in Poland's public enterprises may have fallen significantly less than shown in Table 4.6 which could then contribute to an explanation of unemployment.[9] However, a better understanding requires analysis of the labour and product markets as attempted in the following section.

Regarding developments of the external sides, it was already mentioned that those countries who incurred fiscal deficits, which were not offset by private savings, had corresponding external current account deficits (Bulgaria and Romania). These deficits amplified the jump in external debt to GDP ratios (Table 4.8) caused by the output declines since 1990, which is particularly eminent in the case of Bulgaria who had both the relatively largest cumulative output loss and cumulative current account deficit (measured as per cent of GDP).[10] On the other hand, Romania was in a position to afford current account deficits if a low debt to GDP ratio is accepted as an indicator of affordability. However, Table 4.9 shows that the successful switch of exports to Western European and international markets resulted in substantially declining external debt servicing burdens, as given by the share of service payments in exports.[11] These developments suggest that the recovery would be export-led,

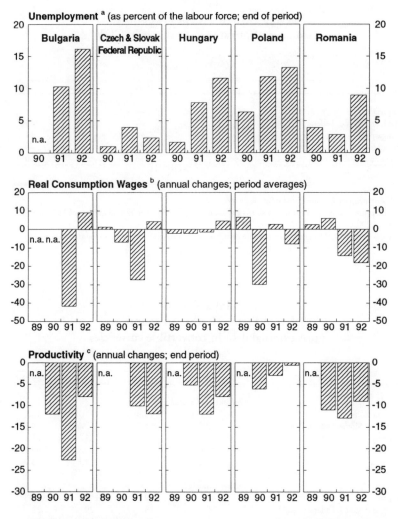

Note: n.a. = not available   *Sources: National sources*

a   1992 figures are estimates.
b   Estimates of real average labour income per employed worker.
c   Productivity figures are estimates based on ratios of real output to total employment.
    Employment figures for 1992 were obtained by deducting estimated unemployment
    from the labour force. The latter was obtained applying average population growth
    during 1989 and 1990 to labour force figures for 1991.

Figure 4.4   Selected Eastern European countries: unemployment, real wages
             and productivity

Table 4.7
Selected Eastern European countries:
estimates of private sector shares in GDP

(As per cent)

	1989	1990	1991
Bulgaria	—	—	—
Czech and Slovak Federal Republic	—	—	9
Hungary a	10	11	11
Poland b	28	35	—
Romania c	15	20	20

Source: International Monetary Fund, Data Fund.

a Using primary income distribution as proxy.
b The primary income distribution shows a share of the private sector in total income of 19% in 1989 and 1990.
c 1989 and 1990: Using primary income distribution as proxy; 1991: Estimate by the authorities.

Table 4.8
Selected Eastern European countries:
gross external debt in convertible currencies

	1989	1990	1991	1992 *
(In billions of U.S. dollars)				
Bulgaria	9.2	10.4	11.7	12.9
Czech and Slovak Federal Republic	7.9	8.2	9.6	9.9
Hungary	20.0	21.3	21.0	21.1
Poland	40.8	49.0	48.4	49.9
Romania	0.8	0.9	1.8	3.9
(As per cent of GDP)				
Bulgaria	42	132	154	134
Czech and Slovak Federal Republic	16	18	29	28
Hungary	68	65	68	65
Poland	61	88	64	59
Romania	3	4	9	24
(As per cent of exports of goods and services in convertible currencies)				
Bulgaria	227	309	280	274
Czech and Slovak Federal Republic	108	101	88	77
Hungary	270	285	216	199
Poland	468	384	325	304
Romaniai	13	27	56	95

Source: International Monetary Fund, Data Fund.

* Estimates.

40

providing a case against fiscal deficits to raise aggregate demand. For the following reasons lower fiscal deficits may promote growth: first, there would be a dampening impact on liberalized interest rates raising investment and thus providing for the increase in productivity required to raise the physical marginal product of labour so as to reduce labour shedding.[12] [13] Second, the resulting even stronger export performance (absorption approach) would alleviate the external debt servicing burden and thus provide for further improvements of the fiscal balance. Third, expectations could be affected such that central banks' credibility in providing for price stability would be enhanced. Thus, the fixed exchange rate policies of the Czech and Slovak Federal Republic and Hungary could become more credible and in Bulgaria, Poland and Romania, where floating exchange rate systems are employed, expectations of devaluations could abate. Such an effect on expectations could significantly moderate wage demands, given that the recent and new experience of relatively high inflation may have eliminated money illusion and given the high degree of openness in all countries with the resulting importance of the import price level for the evolution of the overall price level. Fourth, given the evolution of money and capital markets, where interest rates are formed on the basis of expectations, lower expected fiscal deficits would lower present interest rates reinforcing the direct effect on the interest rate level caused by lower aggregate demand and lower interest expenditures on domestic public debt. Fifth, capital flows could

Table 4.9
Selected Eastern European countries:
external debt service payments

	1989	1990	1991	1992 [a]
(In billions of U.S. dollars)				
Bulgaria [b]	3.0	3.9	2.3	2.1
Czech and Slovak Federal Republic	1.7	1.5	1.7	1.7
Hungary	3.6	4.1	3.9	3.9
Poland	1.6	0.7	3.0	3.4
Romania	2.0	—	—	0.1
(As per cent of exports of goods and services in convertible currencies)				
Bulgaria [b]	74.4	117.3	54.1	44.3
Czech and Slovak Federal Republic	23.1	18.5	15.5	13.5
Hungary	48.2	55.0	40.1	36.5
Poland	17.9	5.8	20.5	20.8
Romania	32.7	1.2	0.4	1.3

Source: International Monetary Fund, Data Fund.

a Estimates.
b Scheduled.

be affected such that foreign direct investment rises and capital outflows diminish, because international capital markets evaluate fiscal performance as one 'economic fundamental.' Sixth, fiscal deficits affect the income distribution. If they are financed inflationary, the result may be for the income distribution to evolve skewed from the outset of the transformation process. If they raise public debt, there will be a transfer from those who pay taxes to those who hold the debt. In addition, the problem of inter-enterprise arrears and non-performing loans in banks' balance sheets will inevitably result in a rise of internal public debt.[14] Present fiscal deficits, that are not inflationary financed, have to be added to the burden of non-performing loans in banks' balance sheets and inter-enterprise arrears.[15] It is for these reasons that fiscal deficits, although they may be meant to improve living standards, could result in the opposite. An additional indication, corroborating the case against fiscal deficits, may be seen in the recent significantly smaller increases or even declines of public capital formation as a share of GDP relative to the increases of the shares of fiscal deficits.[16]

In sum, the period of transition since 1990 resulted in output losses that declined substantially during 1992, suggesting, in connection with the generally strong export performance, an export-led recovery.[17] The following section addresses one cause for the deteriorating fiscal balances (declining public sector enterprise profitability), describes the pursued incomes policies and assesses the evolution of unemployment.

2. Wage and price determination under incomes policy

As noted above, to substantiate the hypothesis the rise in unemployment is attributable to the divergence between real wage levels and productivity, a model of wage and price determination is required, appropriate in representing actual behaviour and, ideally, this model would need to be empirically tested so as to be able to use it in explaining unemployment. The 'corporate governance' problem was identified in the literature as the major obstacle for transition and structural adjustment.[18] This work includes models that aim at deriving the consequences of incomes policy when management is labour controlled. Dependent on assumptions, the consequences are ambiguous. For instance, as shown in Milesi-Ferretti (1992), assuming that the government's real income share is given and hence labour's share is a residual with inflationary financing of the fiscal deficit being the adjustment mechanism to scale down labour's claim, allowing inflation to negatively affect productivity, and making certain further assumptions,[19] a lowering of the wage indexation parameter with an excessive target real wage, could cause instability and accelerated output decline. However, the general conclusion is that increased real wage flexibility improves the economy's performance, confirming that, in theory, incomes policy in the

42

form of wage indexation inhibits adjustment to adverse shocks. Given the uncertainties regarding the behavioral content of an appropriate macroeconomic model, a simple price equation, presented later in this section, confirms three most essential policy implications: barring privatization, private sector growth may be spurred owing to downward pressure on wages which are far below those in trading partner countries, hence lessening the need for demand stimulating interventions, policies promoting competition and transparency are fundamental, and subsidies to public enterprises are endangering the fiscal balance and performance of public enterprises.

Appendix II shows that an integral part of the adopted macroeconomic reform and structural adjustment programs, implemented at the outset of reform in each of the five countries, has been an incomes policy in the form of non-deductibility from public enterprises' and cooperatives' taxable profit of wage increases exceeding a norm and a tax levied on these 'excess' wage increases. The evolving private sectors were either exempted from these regulations (Bulgaria, Poland), or largely exempted (Czech and Slovak Federal Republic, Hungary, Romania).[20] All countries permitted partial indexation of wages to consumer price levels. In Poland indexation was formally introduced in July 1989, in Hungary de facto indexation had been present and in the other three countries indexation was introduced several months after initial price liberalization. All countries used initially the wage bill as the reference point.[21] In response to rising unemployment, Poland switched in 1991 from the wage bill to the average wage. Practical problems with the policy have been tax avoidance through fringe benefits, widespread disregard of the norm and accumulation of tax payments arrears (particularly on the part of those enterprises who are recipients of subsidies dependent on losses), debatable exemptions attempting to permit firm restructuring etc., frequent adjustments and partial forgiveness (owing to fear of social unrest) at the beginning of a year after the norm had been exceeded commonly during the end of the previous year. Hungary abolished the excess wage regulation in 1992 due to fear of allocative costs in terms of hindered wage differentiation. Poland lowered the marginal tax rates in 1992. Wage policy regarding the large share of government employment was generally used as a tool of guidance. As a result, significant spreads between real wages obtained in the three employment spheres public sector, public enterprises and cooperatives, and the private sector emerged.

The rapid adoption of incomes policy in the form of an excess wage increase tax during the reform process indicates that governments anticipated wage determination in public enterprises and cooperatives not to correspond to the evolution of the value of the marginal product of labour. De facto and formal indexation of wages to consumer prices may have contributed to the need for taxing 'excess wages,' particularly in light of the large terms of trade shock. The questions are whether this type of incomes policy was needed to prevent a straight-forward transfer of revenues to workers and whether it was effective.

For Poland, and in accordance with Figure 4.4 and Table 4.6 above, Berg and Blanchard (1992) find that during 1990 managers of state-enterprises behaved neither as profit maximizers nor as labour representatives. The decisions of firms were consistent with a fairly long horizon on the part of workers. Regarding 1991 the evidence may suggest that, despite incomes policy, a redistribution of revenues from profits to wages took place: firms decreased employment by less than ouptut fell and, due to partial indexation of the wage increase norm, wages could be raised in response to the substantial price increases of non-labour inputs (terms of trade shock). This latter fact points to the problematic nature of indexation of nominal wages in general.

Aggregate wage restraint became largely dependent on skills of government officials in negotiations with trade unions, managements, and parliaments: in Bulgaria and in the Czech and Slovak Federal Republic, the institution 'Tripartite Agreements' was established. In Hungary and Romania changes in the indexation coefficient, determining the wage norm, were carried out in consultation with trade unions. In Poland, a 'Pact on Enterprises,' comprising several laws facilitating privatization and providing for the establishment of an advisory Tripartite Commission, was concluded in 1992, following a period during which determination of the norm appears to have been largely dependent upon negotiations with the parliament.

On a theoretical level, important factors as to wage and price setting by firms are control of management by whom, and expectations of employees and managements as to privatization. If management is controlled by employees who fear privatization, the likely result appears to be maximization of income per employee until privatization or bankruptcy, implying no incentive for both to secure a proper yield on capital and hire outsiders. The enterprise's capital stock could be depleted rendering privatization and survival of the firm more difficult. If management is controlled by the government, owing, for instance, to the so-called 'hard budget constraints,' management behaviour depends on whether incentives exist providing for them to view privatization as beneficial for themselves.[22] If these incentives are missing, capital stock depletion could nevertheless occur, even if management has to prove profitability, because the latter may be disguised. Hence, both the marginal efficiency of capital and of labour would decline, resulting in price increases which firms would find infeasible where markets are competitive, so that wages would have to fall. Otherwise, depletion of the capital stock would accelerate due to forgone investment. In all five countries, workers' councils appear to have a significant influence on management, the latter being formally controlled by governments. However, in the Czech and Slovak Federal Republic, Hungary and Poland, clear rules have been established regarding privatization and, as mentioned, in Poland incentives have been strengthened for both employees and managements to view privatization as beneficial. With respect to Bulgaria and Romania it is less clear to which extent Privatization Agencies or managements can privatize without approval by workers' councils. Regarding Eastern European countries where data are available, it appears that investment ratios in public enterprises and cooperatives fell, indicating that it has been difficult for management to seeking a sufficient return on capital. Appendix III simplifies these developments and derives a price equation of the form:

$$(5) \quad \dot{p} = \alpha(\dot{p}^* + \dot{e}) + \beta(\dot{w} - \dot{x} + \dot{m} + \dot{t} + \dot{p}_m^* + \dot{e})$$

$$+ \gamma(\dot{w} - \dot{x} + \dot{m} + \dot{t} + \dot{p}_m + \dot{e})$$

$$\text{with } \alpha + \beta + \gamma = 1$$

Labour productivity is denoted by x, α denotes the weight in the overall price level of price setting by private and public enterprises operating in competitive markets, β denotes the respective weight of private enterprises who have a monopolistic position, and γ is the respective weight of public enterprises in such a position. Dots above variables denote growth rates.

The equation confirms that the larger the degree of openness and hence the larger α, the less firms can push prices to raise wages;[23] the weight of public enterprises with dominant market position may adversely affect price developments. Although subsidies enter the equation with a minus sign, their overall effect on inflation will be neutral when they are inflationary financed. Regarding the effects of the excess wage tax, in the case of private enterprises in a monopolistic position, the tax appears likely to be passed on to buyers by raising the share of monopolistic rent that is extracted; in the case of public enterprises in such a position, it will be offset if subsidies are granted and hence the tax is paid for by taxpayers. Hence, non-deductibility of 'excess' wages and their taxation would probably not succeed in lowering wage growth where competition is insufficient or where subsidies are granted. Only firms subject to a considerable degree of competition would have to reflect on how to circumvent the regulation. The short run impact on the inflation rate of the chosen exchange rate system is also evident. Given the relatively limited shares of private sectors in the considered countries, it would appear that Υ is relatively large. Hence, inflation could accelerate, and income would be redistributed, which may explain why Poland perceived the policy as ineffective and Hungary's abolishment of the tax.

Under certain restrictive assumptions, the evolution of unemployment may be assessed. Private firms account for a certain share in a, the share being assumed to be relatively small. β is accounted for by private firms only, since they do not receive subsidies, and it is assumed that β is also relatively small. Υ is accounted for by public enterprises only. Private firms are assumed to be profit maximizers whereas public firms tend to maximize income per employee. Technology is held constant in all firms. The excess wage tax is assumed to be avoided or offset by subsidies. Subsidies are paid in an amount equal to wage tax revenue. The starting point is a hypothetical equilibrium with no involuntary unemployment, where the real wage paid by public and private firms is given by equations (1) and (2), respectively, as shown in Appendix III. Assuming a disturbance in form of an adverse demand shock regarding goods and services produced by public enterprises, these firms are forced to lower their prices. A fall of the nominal wage would be required to maintain the employment level. If workers' councils resist this move, firms are forced to lay off. Given the assumed negligible size of the private sector, these unemployed will search work in other public enterprises. However, public enterprises would be apprehensive as to hiring additional staff, since this may decrease income per employee. In addition, they may expect a downward shift of the demand curve they face and therefore be even more cautious in hiring. As a result, unemployment emerges. Productivity increases and a growing share of the private sector in total output could raise the employment level. The larger unemployment, the larger could be, *ceteris paribus*, the return private capital receives which could accelerate private sector productivity growth and thus provide an adjustment mechanism to reduce unemployment. Given the planned tax systems which attempt to minimize distortions, this result would not be affected by taxation. However, such a development is likely to cause social conflicts and therefore it could not substitute for creating incentives for workers' councils and managements to seek privatization themselves or through the mentioned other means.[24] Closure of public enterprises that are unviable in the long run would encourage entry of private firms into industries and thus promote growth (Husain, 1992).

Notes

1   The Czech and Slovak Federal Republic and Hungary pegged their currencies to a currency basket, Bulgaria and Romania adopted floating rates, Poland's currency was initially pegged to the U.S. dollar, a policy that was abandoned in favour of an independent float sixteen months after start of reform. Appendix I does not provide detailed information on the specific approaches taken towards privatization and institutional reform. Information on the former is provided in Husain and Sahay (1992) and Hemming (1992).

2   The reasons are various adverse demand and supply shocks: the former result from (i) large required changes in relative prices implying a shift of resources from sectors facing less demand to sectors facing higher demand which, under condition of imperfectly mobile factors of production, requires time; (ii) an increase in interest rates if these are liberalized, (iii) dishoarding of accumulated inventories prior to price liberalization, (iv)

uncertainty affecting consumption and investment. The latter result from (i) difficulties in establishing immediately the institutional framework required to enable the price mechanism to perform its plan coordinating role, (ii) potential disruptions, particularly to the distribution system, (iii) exerted monopoly power of enterprises, (iv) price increases of imported primary inputs. Detailed accounts are provided in Blanchard and Layard (1990), Blanchard and Berg (1992), and Borensztein, Demekas, and Ostry (1992). The evidence regarding the question whether a certain type of shock dominated is mixed. The latter authors find the output decline in Bulgaria, the Czech and Slovak Federal Republic, and Romania to be attributable mainly to supply shocks and to have been associated with little structural change within industrial sectors. For Poland, Berg and Blanchard (1992) and Schaffer (1992) attribute the output decline mainly to demand shocks.

3   The terms of trade shock during 1990 and 1991 appears to have been in the order of 25 to 30 per cent for the five countries, except Hungary, whose terms-of-trade deteriorated significantly less (Table 4.1). Thus, in addition to the actual loss of output and under the assumption for the production structure to have remained unchanged, Bulgaria and Romania, with degrees of openness close to, or above, 100 per cent of GDP, suffered a welfare loss of roughly 25-30 per cent of reduced GDP. Specifically, the resulting decline in the feasible real wage level is dependent upon the weight of import prices in the total price level. The latter is given by:

$$p = \alpha + \beta w + (1-\beta) \, p^*$$

where p is the logarithm of the price level, w is the logarithm of the wage level, p^* is the logarithm of the import price level, β is the weight of wages in the total price level, and α is a constant. Hence, the real wage level equals:

$$w - p = \alpha + [\, (1-\beta) \, / \, \beta \,] \, (p-p^*).$$

To the extent that the shares of imports in GDP may be taken as proxies for $(1-\beta)$, (Bulgaria: 35 per cent, Romania: 61 per cent, both in 1989), the feasible real wage was reduced, *ceteris paribus*, and assuming an increase of import prices by 25 per cent with no change in export prices, by 13 per cent in Bulgaria and 39 per cent in Romania. This underlines the importance of adjustment of the production structure and capital stock to the new relative prices so as to increase the feasible real wage level. As mentioned above, a tariff could provide relief and raise welfare immediately, but it would, first, prevent full integration into world markets and thus reduce the long run welfare gains for the Eastern European countries from trade, second, conserve concentration, and third, cause additional costs if it were to be abolished at a later time.

4 Table 4.2 shows that prior to transition, this degree had been relatively high by international standards with the ratios of the sum of exports and imports to GDP ranging from 32 per cent, in the case of Poland, to 112 per cent in the case of Bulgaria. Openness was maintained during transition.

5 Poland took these measures already during the latter half of 1989 and during 1990. The Czech and Slovak Federal Republic, followed in the beginning of 1991, Bulgaria, Hungary and Romania liberalized most prices in the course of 1991. Price controls or subsidized prices remain in all countries and concern mainly household energy and some raw materials.

6 During 1991 and 1992 all countries were forced to provide the banking system and public enterprises with capital injections or loans, in an attempt to halt the deterioration of banks' balance sheets due to rising, although non-performing, loans to these enterprises. The outlays were, however, not included in the budgets but raised public debt or public guarantee obligations. Estimates of these expenditures in 1991 are as follows (ratios to GDP): Bulgaria: 11 per cent, Czech and Slovak Federal Republic: 5 per cent, Poland: 2.9 per cent (inter-enterprise arrears in 1991 were estimated to have stood at 23 per cent of GDP), Romania: 12.5 per cent.

7 To establish a relationship between real wages, productivity and unemployment, a theory is required. If markets were competitive, then the aggregate real wage level would equal the aggregate marginal product of labour and involuntary unemployment could not arise. If labour is organized and product markets are competitive, then involuntary unemployment rises with the aggregate real wage level exceeding the aggregate marginal product. If product markets are monopolistic and labour is organized, then unemployment may arise if the real wage level exceeds the marginal product plus monopolistic rent. If firms are labour managed, then unemployment is inherent, because firms maximize income of employed persons implying that there are no incentives to hire new staff. Hence, the need for a model that appears appropriate under present circumstances as discussed in the following section.

8 The evolution of unemployment differs largely in the Czech and Slovak Republics.

9 As explained above, real wage developments do not permit an inferance as to the evolution of living standards. Regarding Poland, opinion polls indicate a rise of living standards even during the initial phase of stabilization when real wages fell sharply (Lipton and Sachs, 1990).

10 In early 1990 Bulgaria declared a debt service payments moratorium and since then serviced external debt partially.

11 The relative decline of Romania's payments is, however, due to the nearly elimination of external debt in 1989.

12 Spreads between lending and deposit rates have been exceptionally high, mainly due to relatively large shares in banks' balance sheets of non-performing loans. Hence, to facilitate a rapid built-up of physical capital through private investment, lower interest rates through lower domestic demand caused by reduced fiscal deficits could be called for.

13 Fiscal deficits raise aggregate demand only, and crowd out private investment, if Ricardian equivalence does not hold. Given the degree of foresight the Ricardian equivalence hypothesis requires, Blanchard (1990, p. 16) dismisses it. Under present conditions of probably still pronounced uncertainty, it may be unreasonable to assume private households to discount properly the future tax burden resulting from current fiscal deficits. The rising private savings ratios in the Czech and Slovak Federal Republic and Hungary should not be seen as being caused by fiscal deficits and thus associated with such discounting behaviour. Rather, they should be seen as an indication of the willingness of individual provisioning and investment oriented behaviour. Proof of this hypothesis is missing. Means to provide it would be a poll or econometric testing if sufficient data were available.

14 The internal public debt to GDP ratios vary widely in the five Eastern European countries. In centrally planned economies fiscal deficits were mainly financed through seignorage, raising excess demand, and credit from the banking system. In addition, Hungary issued public bonds and treasury bonds for several years prior to transition. Hence, to arrive at the internal public debt figures, the stock of net credit to the government sector provided by the banking system and bonds issued by the public sector need to be added. The resulting public debt to GDP ratios (excluding public enterprises) are approximately (end of 1991): Bulgaria: 37 per cent, Czech and Slovak Federal Republic: 11 per cent (excluding Consolidation Bank and including Kcs 50 billion bond issue by National Property Fund), Hungary: 35 per cent, Poland: 17 per cent, Romania: 18 per cent (including lei 426 billion net credit extended under 'global compensation' scheme completed January 1992).

15 This latter problem appears to have been resolved, to a large extent, in the Czech and Slovak Republic and Hungary, and to some extent in Romania (Appendix I, column 1992). If it was legitimate to regard inter-enterprise arrears in Poland at end 1991 as an indication of the future rise in public debt due to this problem and also regarding Bulgaria, then an increase of at least 25 per cent of GDP in public domestic debt would result.

16 The above reasoning considers the major relationships only. The mechanisms at work are more complicated with expectations assuming a crucial role. For instance, private capital formation in an open economy (the decisive variable in determining the future growth path) may be assumed to be primarily dependent upon expected relative profits. Hence, as mentioned above by referring to Giavazzi and Pagano (1990), presently high taxation,

high fiscal deficits and high inflation may not be detrimental to growth if policy changes are expected. Given the importance of public investment in infrastructure, it could be argued that capital expenditures may be financed through domestic and/or foreign borrowing. To avoid potential abuse, Bruno (1992) suggests to provide both a definition of these expenditures and a limit in terms of GDP or share of the fiscal deficit. Given that several years may pass before a personal income tax and VAT (introduced or planned in all countries) will provide orderly revenues, the issue of optimal financing arises. Bruno (1992) suggests to consider temporary increases in tariffs. (As of December 1992, Poland introduced a 6 per cent import surcharge and increased other tax rates). This, however, raises the issues of highly concentrated domestic markets and the effect on the physical capital stock associated with raising the relatively low tariffs. Capital markets are underdeveloped and only the Czech and Slovak Federal Republic and Romania have relatively low total public debt to GDP ratios (estimated at end 1992 at about 45 per cent and 40 per cent, respectively, where uncertainty regarding these and the following ratios, which exclude inter-enterprise arrears, is large). Bulgaria's, Hungary's, and Poland's total public debt to GDP ratio at end 1992 are estimated at about 200 per cent, 110 per cent and 90 per cent, respectively.

17 A consequence of the large output declines and obsolescence of much of the capital stock are relatively low capital-labour ratios. Hence, the marginal product of capital may be expected to be relatively large, promoting growth. Using a production function that accounts for physical capital, human capital (high school enrollment) and labour, Borensztein and Montiel (1992) calculate annual real growth rates for the Czech and Slovak Federal Republic, Hungary and Poland which could amount to about 4, 6, and 8 per cent, respectively, in the medium-term (5 years). Poland's relatively more favorable growth prospect stems from a lower initial capital stock. These estimates do not account, however, for political stability.

18 See, for instance, Lipton and Sachs (1990), Hinds (1991), Lane and Dinopoulos (1991), Lane (1991), Berg and Blanchard (1992), Bruno (1992), Dinopoulos and Lane (1992), Milesi-Ferretti (1992), Husain (1992).

19 His models take employment as exogenous.

20 The details of the policies are presented in Appendix II.

21 Using the wage bill rather than average wages would be expected to encourage labour shedding and hinder expansion. However, Lane (1991) shows that even if the wage bill and not the average wage is subject to an incomes policy, a labour managed firm (assumed to maximize expected utility of workers) may choose higher employment. Major assumptions in deriving this result are that utility depends only on consumption and that capital

markets are underdeveloped so that there is no way to diversify away risk associated with employment. However, with unemployment benefits and the enterprise profits tax rate rising, *ceteris paribus*, the incentive to choose higher employment declines.

22 Incentives in the form of long-maturity stock options and/or a long-term profit share in the manager's contract are suggested by Bruno (1992). He also points to the political stalemate between workers' councils and managements which could be resolved through giveaway schemes making both parties beneficiaries of privatization. This latter method has successfully been applied in the Czech and Slovak Federal Republic where vouchers could be invested either directly in enterprises or through the intermediary of 'Investment Privatization Funds,' and in Poland where legislation introduced in 1992, the 'Pact on Enterprises,' provided for employees of state enterprises to receive 10 per cent of the enterprise's stock free of charge.

23 The problem of market structure is thus fundamental. Anti-trust laws in industrial countries are adapted continuously to the evolution of markets.

24 Husain and Sahay (1992) show that if privatization proceeds slowly, and assuming that over the period of privatization shocks to demand of final goods dominate those to supply of primary goods, efficiency gains could be achieved by first privatizing final goods industries. Intuitively, this results if one accepts that private firms are more flexible in responding to market signals.

5 Evaluation of incomes policy in selected Eastern European countries

The review of the theoretical analysis of incomes policy showed there is only one viable case for incomes policy, namely inflationary inertia when inflation is high. Empirical analysis corroborates this conclusion, if incomes policy is defined narrowly as here. According to Figure 4.2, inflation was substantially reduced (except in Romania), and all countries aim at restrictive monetary policy not permitting fiscal deficits to be financed through money creation. The established Central Banks in the Czech and Slovak Federal Republic and Hungary were granted relative independence, giving credibility to this aim. As explained previously, restrictive policies may affect expectations such that the immediate impact on growth is positive, provided they are consistent and thus credible. Incomes policy may interfere with this consistency, namely when it is not evaluated in the average assessment of market participants as effective and if restrictive policies become therefore less credible. Therefore, the case for incomes policy based on inertia appears to be weak. May it be argued that a second case arises due to transition? Theoretical analysis is inconclusive, mainly due to uncertainty as to the appropriate modelling of public enterprise management behaviour. The argumentation may therefore be based on actual developments. These show that firms reacted either by avoiding the excess wage tax, mainly through fringe benefits, or, particularly in cases were enterprises receive subsidies, by tax payment. Governments granted exemptions and in some instances forgave the tax partially. Avoidance supports the hypothesis for incomes policy not to be enforceable. Government behaviour underlines failures in the policy process. The controls failed to prevent declines in profits, because employment was reduced by less than output fell, and because partial indexation of the wage increase norm permitted rising non-labour input costs to translate into higher wages. However, managements and workers' councils could not be expected to seeking a sufficient return on capital during the output decline as long as incentives were insufficient for them to regard privatization as beneficial for themselves. Had these incentives been strong enough, the need for incomes policy may not have arisen. If it is held that the policy process did not permit immediate establishment of sufficiently strong incentives, then transition appears to provide a case for incomes policy as a means to promote adjustment and halt capital stock depletion. However, as described above, several countries strengthened measures apt to solve the 'corporate governance' problem and thus to ensuring that managements of state enterprises seek a proper return on capital. Hence, the benefits of incomes policy decline while the costs of it may remain unchanged.

Another problem associated with incomes policy during transition may be considered. If pursued over a fairly long period and applied only to public enterprises as a substitute for privatization incentives, it could create tensions due to perceived unfairness. If applied to both private and public sectors and assuming it is successful in achieving wage restraint, it would, *ceteris paribus*, contribute to a further deviation of productivity growth differentials: the private sectors may not face a problem of wage inflation, given these differentials and unemployment. Therefore, either way, transition could make it more difficult for incomes policy to be sustainable.

Given the indications for real growth to be likely to resume in the short term, incomes policy, if envisaged by the authorities to be maintained in whatever form, may be evaluated within a broader context than facilitating adjustment of real wages in line with decreasing marginal products of labour and capital. This context may be seen in Eichner and Kregel's (1975) conclusion for an inflationary process to be caused by distributional conflict. The empirical evidence appears to suggest that those industrial countries who achieved this conflict to be settled within institutions experienced relatively stable growth, higher than the industrial countries' average, and relatively low inflation (e.g. Austria, Japan, Germany, Switzerland). Particularly in Japan, real wages responded relatively flexible to adverse external shocks. This lends support to modelling inflation as a positive function of distributional conflict and growth as a negative function of inflation.[1] Conflict contributes to inflation resulting in less growth. Classical theory assumes perfect competition, implying the income distribution to be determined by the marginal productivities of labour and capital. Conflict is prevented due to lack of ability to increase the own income share other than through higher productivity. With Dalziel (1990, p. 427) this ability (market power) may be defined as '... setting the current price (wage) level without its value .. being used by workers (firms) when setting the current wage (price) level.' In other words, market power arises if only one party has certainty. In reality, labour and capital have market power (which takes turns, perhaps mainly related to the economy's position in the business cycle) and can pursue excessive income claims resulting in the income distribution oscillating. A first best solution would be to eliminate market power through open markets. But competition may be enforced only to a degree where incentives to win a comparative advantage are not weakened.[2] Therefore, these policies are not sufficient to reduce conflict. Institutions are needed to internalize conflict preferably without involvement of the government. The creation of such institutions begins at organization of wage bargaining. If wages are not determined by collective bargaining, then they should be determined unilaterally by the employer (e.g. United States), because decentralized bargaining with relatively powerful trade unions proved to be inconsistent with low unemployment (e.g. United Kingdom) (Layard, 1990, 1991)). Centralized bargaining proved to be consistent with low unemployment provided employers' federations and trade unions are well coordinated among themselves and negotiate at their highest levels resulting in national coordination.[3] The Scandinavian experience suggests that joint economic analysis prior to bargaining reduces conflict. In addition, Eastern European countries may be at an advantage due to relatively small size so that Austria's 'Parity Commission' with few members could provide an example.[4] Another level would be regulation of unemployment compensation. If the system has a relatively high retention ratio and benefits are granted with long duration, then incentives should be introduced for unemployed to seek training and jobs and for wage bargaining parties to consider unemployment, for instance, through a shift in the split of social security contributions among employers and employees.[5]

The following scenario, considering an Eastern European economy, may illustrate the role of an institutional set-up conducive to growth. The assumptions are: (i) the external sector grows relatively fast, owing to both less expensive labour than in competitor countries and subdued domestic demand (due to precautionary savings and unemployment). Therefore its relative size is large; (ii) wage inflation is present providing for an overall inflation rate above the average rate of main competitors; (iii) incomes policy is not pursued. Under these conditions, an economy with a pegged exchange rate (Czech and Slovak Federal Republic, Hungary) could experience a profit squeeze in the external sector. As noted above, dependent on the established unemployment compensation system, the wage equation may incorporate a term representing higher than 'natural' unemployment. It may also incorporate a term representing the degree of credibility bargainers attach to the fixed exchange rate policy. With the government's announced measures or strategies being evaluated by markets, on average, as time consistent and thus credible, and with the central bank being independent, pursuing no other objective than inflation,[6] the pegged exchange rate will, *ceteris paribus* and as evaluated by the average market participant, tend to become credible. Both terms could be expected to dampen wage inflation if social conflict does not interfere. Given policies securing open markets, a system of wage bargaining that reduces conflict prior to bargaining (for instance by means of joint economic forecasting) and an institution to which income claims are directed in case bargaining yields no result within a period stipulated by law (e.g. parity commission, mediator), conflict may be expected to be absorbed. In addition, there should be a mechanism which ensures that income claims by special interest groups do not result in regulations favoring them except by way of the parliamentary process. Policies promoting competition make a prisoner's dilemma less likely. Hence, to the extent that policies are credible and markets open, movement towards Nash-equilibrium is promoted containing wage inflation and the external sector's profit squeeze without incomes policy.

In an economy with a floating exchange rate (Bulgaria, Poland, Romania), wage bargaining parties could expect currency depreciations to provide a remedy to wage inflation. To the extent that depreciations become trivial, dependent on inflationary expectations, pressure on firms' competitiveness could lessen and so may efforts to improve productivity.[7] Profit margins may therefore decline despite depreciations. (This would also undermine monetary policy's short run relative efficacy). Moreover, accomodation of changes in relative prices among countries by exchange rate policy may result in higher persistence of relative inflation rates: the accommodating policy could lead market participants to expect lower unemployment which would result in higher expected current and future nominal wages, which, in turn, and under the assumption of convex costs of adjusting prices, would cause inertia of price increases (Alogoskoufis and Smith, 1991; Alogoskoufis, 1992). Hence, a flexible exchange rate regime could contribute to a permanently higher domestic inflation rate than would be the case under a system of an adjustable peg. Without a target for exchange rate movements and unstable money demand, an inflation target for the central bank is rendered difficult to achieve.[8] Therefore, in this system creation of the above described institutions appears inevitable, so as to provide a substitute for the missing 'anchor' for the economy's nominal magnitudes and for macroeconomic policy, which would also serve to prevent the government from becoming distracted from responsibility for time consistent policy.[9]

Taking into account the multitude of measures available to strengthen incentives to privatize and to provide for orderly management of public sector enterprises, some of which have been implemented in several of the studied countries, it may be concluded that transition to a market economy does not appear to provide a case for incomes policy.

Notes

1   See, in particular, Turnovsky and Pitchford (1978) and Dalziel (1990).
2   It may be noted that increasing market transparency is one aspect of policies promoting competition. Privatization could be associated with externalities (for instance, lower wages due to unemployment, acquisition of assets below market value). Transition thus strengthens the general case

for government action to improve transparency. Dooley and Isard (1992) suggest establishment of a Planning Agency who would support market mechanisms. Transparency improvement could, however, also be the responsibility of the anti-trust agency.

3   Centrally coordinated wage determination would endow trade unions with excessive power if managements are labour controlled. This may be seen as supporting the decision of the former Czech and Slovak Federal Republic to have implemented credible steps towards privatization in the beginning of transition.

4   Austria's Parity Commission comprises the Government. There may be reservations to such an organization, because involvement of the government bears the danger of interference with consistent policies. For instance, participation of the government could lead to tax concessions and this may result in further regulations detrimental to consistency.

5   Employers could be charged most of the contributions needed to finance pensions, while employees would bear most of the cost of unemployment compensation with the shares of both groups in total social security contributions remaining unchanged.

6   Kydland and Prescott (1977) argue that if the central bank's objective function contains an employment target and the institution perceives markets to evaluate its policy as credible, then it could be tempted to pursue expansionary policy so as to achieve that employment target and thus risk credibility. The preferable way in achieving an inflation target during transition is the choice of an exchange rate target, given that pursuance of a monetary target is rendered difficult due to instability of money demand and uncertainty regarding potential growth. Lane (1992) finds for Poland that the variance of exchange rate changes (parallel market) had a significant positive impact, and their covariance with inflation a significant negative impact on the demand for money in the 1980s. Interpreted together, these two findings confirm that reducing inflation and variance of the exchange rate will increase demand for money and make it more stable, the effect being probably reinforced on account of substantial unofficial foreign currency holdings. Hence, monetary targeting, if preferred on account of the welfare gain which adherence to simple rules may afford due to enhanced credibility of policies, could be envisaged for the medium-run, and given expected rapid real output growth, seignorage would increase, providing some direct (limited) relief for the fiscal balance.

7   A comparison of the productivity evolution during the 1980s regarding tradeables sectors with a large relative size in countries, on the one hand, whose currency was subject to continuous appreciation with that in countries who, on the other, experienced currency depreciation, appears to suggest that external sector productivity and evolution of the exchange rate are related. Specifically, during this period, Japan's external sector produc-

tivity growth outweighed wage increases and partly offset appreciation. Since productivity growth was associated with product quality improvements, export prices could be raised resulting in some increase in the aggregate profit margin. Productivity growth in Germany has been less strong, but was sufficient to offset wage growth. By contrast, Greece, employing a flexible exchange rate regime and having a relatively large external sector, experienced nearly continuous depreciations concomitant with external sector productivity growth less than would have been required to maintain the aggregate profit margin.

8   Credit ceilings for individual banks proved to be a hindrance, because they discouraged banks' deposit taking. In addition, they are an important element of discretionary policies bearing the risk of arbitrariness and may violate efficient resource allocation.

9   One may argue that there is no inherent need for a nominal 'anchor.' Central banks could keep the price level constant by raising and lowering the interest rate level above and below its 'natural' rate, as originally suggested by Wicksell and Keynes. Given, however, that views regarding the 'natural' rate may differ, the central bank could be placed under significant pressure, suggesting this argument to be not of practical use.

6 Summary and concluding remarks

Incomes policy, if not meant to break inflationary inertia or defined as planning-subordinated policy creating institutions that internalize distributional conflict, appears to be subject to an error of logic, because a transaction has an infinite number of dimensions undermining enforceability. Incomes policy is no substitute for restrictive fiscal and monetary policy, because it is distortive and only the latter two can achieve lasting improvement of the fiscal balance and inflation. It may even promote expansionary policy when authorities believe in its effectiveness. Appeals to self-denying behaviour contradict entrepreneurship which is the cause for productivity growth and the foundation of a market economy. Tax-based incomes policy causes an array of distortions, in particular, it can be considered an indirect tax on investment, possibly hindering growth. The empirical evidence regarding industrial countries suggests that incomes policy has involved governments in wage bargaining to an extent that responsibility for an undistortive, equitable, and efficient tax system and consistent demand management was undermined. As any policy recommendation, a proposal of an incomes policy should consider failures in the policy process. The experience Eastern European countries had with exemptions, partial forgiveness and abolishment of the excess wage increase tax resembles that of the United States, where two of four attempts to pursue incomes policy appear to have failed due to presidential intervention in 'favour' of trade unions. In some Western European countries, incomes policy entailed further interventions in production and consumption and, in one instance, evidently promoted decentralized wage bargaining which proved not to be consistent with low unemployment if trade unions are relatively influential. Additional costs of incomes policy may arise due to weakened incentives to work, invest and save. Remaining major obstacles for Eastern European economies to grow rapidly may be seen in slowly proceeding privatization or liquidation of public enterprises, particularly those of large size, and improvements of the institutional framework, especially with regard to the tax system, tax administration and control of market structures. As long as employees and managements were apprehensive towards privatization, transition may have provided a case for incomes policy, if there was no other means available to prevent potential capital stock depletion. However, the recorded evolution of unemployment during 1990 through 1992, subject to considerable qualifications, appears to be related to the one of real wages, indicating that missing incentives for workers and managements contributed to a transfer of revenues to workers despite incomes policy. Incomes policy has been largely ineffective and it could promote either, productivity differentials in the private and public sectors if applied to both, or tensions if applied only to public enterprises. Therefore, it cannot be regarded as a substitute for strengthening incentives to privatize. Several Eastern European countries improved substantially incentive structures, indicating that the 'corporate governance' problem is being solved. The relationship between unemployment and real wages also points to the problematic nature of wage indexation in general. It may contribute to unemployment.

A society should reflect on how to cope with distributional conflict so as to prevent inflation becoming the means to scale down nominal income claims which may be costly. Incomes policy appears not to be a solution to conflict, because it is theoretically unsustainable what has been proven empirically and what may be underlined due to transition. One prospect could be for the income distribution to evolve skewed, provided the aggregate profit margins of the evolving private sectors reflect wage differentials to competitor countries and the planned tax systems will not be modified. Another prospect could be for unemployment to evolve as it has in many industrial countries, namely dependent on its history. Fiscal deficits would contribute to skeweness and hinder growth, largely independent of their financing: if they raise domestic public debt, they are likely to slow down formation of the physical capital stock and thus growth of output and employment. If they raise external debt, growth may be inhibited when the domestic return on the funds is below the foreign interest rate. If they raise inflation, distortions are created and expectations of domestic and foreign market participants are adversely affected, implying also a negative impact on growth. It appears that neither skeweness nor unemployment could be alleviated by incomes policy. Distributional conflict could therefore intensify. Galbraith (1952) stated that it was not for lack of theoretical foundation or for lack of administrability that controls programs would not be implemented, but for lack of political will. With restrictive policies, incentives introduced for managements and workers' councils to view privatization as beneficial for themselves, institutions established providing for both internalization of income distributional disputes, preferably without involvement of the government, and open markets, it may appear legitimate to cite Rakowski (1983): 'In a society which aspires to be free and efficient, what role is there for [wage(*author's insertion*)] controls?'

Appendix I
Selected Eastern European countries: major macro-economic reform measures

Bulgaria

1990	1991	1992

March
Declaration of a debt servicing moratorium.

May
Adoption of a fixed exchange rate system based on three exchange rates.

September
Fund membership under Article XIV status.

January
Introduction of unified corporate profit tax rate set at 40%

February
Adoption of economic reform programme to stabilize and restructure the economy.

Pillars
Price and external trade liberalization; privatization and commercialization of public enterprises; tight fiscal and monetary policy; floating exchange rate system; tax-based incomes policy; interest rate liberalization; reform of tax system; land reform; institutional reform.

December
Restitution laws covering small firms, residential and industrial property.

General
Implementation of interest rate liberalization. Partial reform of tariff system (including introduction of a minimum import tariff rate of 5% with no exemptions).
Demonopolization of conglomorates in the industrial and services sectors.

January
New foreign investment law providing for liberalized foreign direct investment.

February
New Laws on the National Bank of Bulgaria providing for its relative independence and on commercial banks which are to operate as universal banks. Admission of foreign banks.

July
New tariff schedule with minimum tariff rate remaining at 5% and most tariffs in the range of 8-17%.

General
Reduction of total subsidies to about 3% of GDP. Laws on enterprise profit tax, value added tax (to replace turnover tax), income tax, and tax administration to become effective January 1993. Privatization Law regulating privatization of enterprises of any size. Detailed implementation programme regarding restitution of land ownership and privatization of land. (Private ownership in housing has traditionally been established).
Regarding issue of inter-enterprise arrears, establishment of Finance Ministry working group. Regarding enterprise indebtedness to banks adoption of strategy to gradually substitute non-performing loans by government bonds and prudential regulatory framework for commercial banks corresponding to international standards.

Czech and Slovak Federal Republic

1990	1991	1992

1990

September
Fund membership under Article XIV status.

General
Formulation of strategy for systemic reform.

Pillars
Price and external trade liberalization; privatization of public enterprises; tight fiscal and monetary policy; pegged exchange rate system (with the koruna pegged to a basket of convertible currencies); tax-based incomes policy; interest rate liberalization; reform of tax system; reform of social security net; institutional reform.

General
Creation of universal banking system. Removal of retail food subsidies. Increases in interest rates. Two devaluations.

1991

January
Price and trade liberalization.

February
Profits and dividends made fully remittable.

August
Import quotas imposed on several agricultural goods and coal. Restitution laws covering small businesses, residential and land ownership.

December
Association agreement with the European Communities providing, among others, for liberalized trade.

General
Privatization of about half of the total of small enterprises (equivalent to about 25,000). Reduction of standard rate of enterprise profits tax to 50%. Introduction of personal incomes tax. Reduction of rates of the turnover tax to four.

1992

January
Revised customs tariff providing for a trade-weighted average rate of 5% (and an average rate of 6%). Replacement of import quotas by automatic licensing system to stem subsidized imports particularly from the EC.

February
New State Bank Law (providing for relative independence of the State Bank of the Czech and Slovak Republic) and law on universal commercial banks.

General
Continued price and trade liberalization. Privatization of about 2,500 enterprises. Reduction of temporary import surcharge on consumer goods to 10%. Reduction of total subsidies to about 5% of GDP. Regarding enterprise indebtedness to banks, prior to privatization, banks received a capital injection of about 5% of GDP to be used mainly for writing down enterprise debt.

Hungary *

* Fund membership 1982 under Article XIV status.

1990	1991	1992

1990

September
Privatization of best performing public enterprises.

November
Adoption of a medium-term macroeconomic reform programme.

Pillars
Price and external trade liberalization; commercialization and privatization of public enterprises; land reform; pegged exchange rate system (forint pegged to a currency basket of convertible currencies); tight fiscal and monetary policy; tax-based incomes policy; interest rate liberalization; continued reform of tax system (initiated in 1988); reform of social security net; institutional reform.

1991

January
Share of liberalized imports raised to about 87% (imports of capital goods from convertible currency area were liberalized in 1989). About 90% of prices comprising the consumer price index liberalized. Initiation of bankrupcy proceedings regarding enterprises in arrears to internal revenue service or social security system for more than three months. Prudential regulatory framework for commercial banks corresponding to international standards.

November
Devaluation of the forint.

December
Partnership treaty with the European Communities providing, among others, for liberalized trade.

General:
Initiation of programme for privatization of State enterprises. New Central Bank Law providing for relative independence of the National Bank of Hungary. Shift to indirect means of monetary control. Liberalization of deposit and lending interest rates.

1992

General
Continued import liberalization (only a negligible share of imports and industrial production remain subject to licensing and/or quotas). Broadening of personal income tax and enterprise profits tax (to include fringe benefits). (No change in the value added tax whose top rate is 25%). Increase of the overall contribution rate for the Solidarity Fund (that finances unemployment benefits) raised from 2 to 6% of the wage bill to reduce transfers from state budget. (Overall social security contribution rate raised to 60% of wages, of which 49% is paid by employer and 11% by employee). Revision of unemployment benefits. Dividend tax rate payable by state enterprises raised to 25%. Reduction of total subsidies to about 5% of GDP. Regarding issue of inter-enterprise arrears, adoption of new laws on bankruptcy and accounting, and requirement for all enterprises not already privatized to be transformed into corporations, and establishment of supervisory authority. Regarding enterprise indebtedness to banks, reliance on new capital adequacy requirements (consistent with Bank for International Settlements' standards implemented internationally) in connection with improved provisoning requirements for doubtful loans and further accounting rules.

Poland *

* Poland rejoined the Fund June 1986 under Article XIV status.

1990	1991	1992
Implementation of major measures aiming at transforming and stabilizing the economy according to systemic reform strategy adopted in 1989.	*January* Constitutional Tribunal (CT) rules that several measures contained in amendments to 1991 Budget Act are unconstitutional. Restrictions on availability of foreign exchange for current account transactions largely eliminated. New external trade contracts denominated in convertible currencies. Removal of limits on repatriation of profits from foreign direct investment.	*January* Personal income tax (with marginal rates set at 20, 30, and 40%) replaces range of taxes on income and wages. Turnover tax introduced with an average rate of 20%.

Pillars
Price and external trade liberalization; commercialization and privatization of public enterprises; pegged exchange rate system following devaluation (with the zloty pegged to the U.S. dollar); tight fiscal and monetary policy; tax-based incomes policy; interest rate liberalization; reform of tax system; reform of social security net; institutional reform.

July
Consolidation of land holdings. Revision of the Law on Employment providing for tightening of access to unemployment benefits. Privatization Law for state-owned enterprises.

May
Devaluation of the zloty and adoption of a crawling peg exchange rate system with the zloty pegged to a basket of currencies.

July
New foreign investment law provides for liberalized foreign direct investment.

General
Enterprise income tax, with rate set at 40%, replaced previous sector-specific enterprise tax.

February
CT rules that aspects of 1991 Budget Act concerning indexation of pensions and other measures are unconstit-ional. General rate for financing the social insurance system (through employer payroll contributions) raised from 43 to 45%.

March
Unemployment compensation restricted.

December
Surcharge on imports of 6%. Additional marginal rate of personal income tax set at 50%. Average turnover tax rate raised by 3 percentage points.

General
Value-added tax (with basic rate set at 22%) planned to replace turnover tax by January 1993.
"Pact on Enterprises" provides for establishment of advisory Tripartite Commission and legislation facilitating privatization.
Regarding issue of inter-enterprise arrears and enterprise indebtedness to banks adoption of strategy focusing on improving incentive structure faced by enterprises and banks, establishment of joint-stock compa-

Poland

(continued)

1990	1991	1992
		nies contracted out to management firms possibly with foreign partners, restructuring or liquidation of unsound enterprises, establishment of "Intervention Fund" dealing with selected enterprises whose liquidation appears socially unfeasible, strengthening of commercial banks through recapitalization, improved management, and new regulatory and supervisory framework.

Romania *

* Fund Membership 1972 under Article XIV status.

1990	1991	1992

1990

Adoption of a medium-term macroeconomic reform programme.

Pillars
Price and external trade liberalization; commercialization and privatization of public enterprises; flexible but managed exchange rate regime; tight fiscal and monetary policy; tax-based incomes policy; interest rate liberalization; land reform; reform of tax system; reform of social security net; institutional reform.

November
Partial price liberalization.

December
Creation of banking system with state and private universal banks headed by the National Bank of Romania. Imposition of bank-specific credit ceilings.

1991

January
Liberalization of imports and exports of goods and services. Certain imports and exports are subject to temporary quotas.

2April
Interest rate liberalization.

May
New foreign direct investment law provides for liberalized foreign direct investment and repatriation of profits.

August
Privatization Law for commercialized enterprises. State Ownership Fund to be established by July 1992 which will receive 70% of share capital with the remaining 30% to be transferred to five private ownership funds. Starting in May 1992 certificates of ownership of the private funds to be distributed in bearer-form, free of charge, to citizens, and tradable in stock market. The State Ownership Fund is required to reduce its share holdings by 10% annually.

October
Elimination of ban-specific credit ceilings.

November
Adoption of unified managed floating exchange rate.

General
Elimination of quantitative import retsrictions. Steady reduction of number of products subject to export quotas and increase of quota limits. Sale of public housing units. Start of land reform.

1992

January
New tariff code provides for a weighted average tariff rate of about 12% (the average rate amounts to about 5%).
Tax reform: simplification of turnover and enterprise profit tax schedules with enterprise profits being taxed progressively up to 45%. (Agricultural incomes are tax exempt). Intention to replace turnover tax by value-added tax in 1993 and other schedular taxes by global income tax in 1994.

May
Reduction of subsidies (amounting to about 4.7% of GDP in 1992) and adoption of plan for their abolishment by end-1993 (excluding subsidies to enterprises).

General
Initiatian of commercialization of some 6,000 state enterprises. Sales of some 5,600 commercialized small-and medium-sized units. 257,000 authorizations for private entrepreneurial activity. Move to indirect means of monetary control. Prices of 16 consumer goods raised that remained controlled. Completion of price liberalization planned for end-1993. Adoption of forward-looking wage indexation policy to promote real wage adjustment. Measures aiming at eliminating built-up of inter-enterprise arrears: "Global Compensation" (completed January 1992) providing for government guaranteed loans from

Romania

(continued)

1990	1991	1992
		banks to enterprises in the amount of their arrears (with net credit extended under this programme equivalant to about 12.5% of GDP of which about 40% refinanced by the National Bank of Romania, the remainder being financed by banks), system to monitor financial situation of enterprises on a monthly basis, early application of bankruptcy procedures, requirement for state owned enterprises to charge market interest on inter-enterprise credits (to be monitored), introduction of a competition law, and bank supervision.

Appendix II
Selected Eastern European countries: adopted incomes policies

Bulgaria

1989	1990	1991	1992

General

Each enterprise allowed to set its own wage bill, subject to a steeply progressive tax on aggregate increases, ranging from marginal rates of 60 to 850%.

September

Indexation of wages, pensions, family allowances, and other types of money incomes on the basis of a monthly consumer price index representing the "social minimum" basket.

Cost of living adjustments are to be made regularly every six months, but could also be triggered whenever the cumulative rise in the price index exceeds 10%, the rate of compensation is 100% for low wages, but averages 50%.

Cost of living adjustments in the fourth quarter, to compensate for a 16% rise in the price index in the third quarter, were not granted.

January

Tripartite agreement on "social peace" among the Government, labour unions, and employers' organizations stipulates that wage increases by more than leva 270 are not generally allowed in the first quarter of 1991. During subsequent quarters, regarding State enterprises and cooperations, ceilings are placed on increases in wage bills on a cumulative quarterly basis compared with a year earlier. Regarding general government employees, wages are adjusted quarterly on the basis of the excess of the actual over-estimated change of the social minimum basket. Private sector wages freely determined.

General

New quarterly ceiling on state sector wage bill intended to keep real wage bill constant.

Czech & Slovak Federal Republic

1989	1990	1991	1992
Wages centrally determined.	*January* Basic wages centrally determined; enterprises can pay bonuses + premia up to 10% of basic wages. If personnel costs exceed the level in the plan, tax of 200% is levied on excess; if growth of average wages (excl. other personnel costs) > 3%, tax is levied ranging from 50% of excess (if between 3 and 4%) to 200% (above 6%).	*January* General Agreement among the Government, employers, and trade unions provides for guidelines regarding wage increases during 1991 consistent with a decline of the aggregate real wage level by 10% (during quarter II-IV) compared to end of 1990. (Limits on nominal wages: Jan.-Feb.: 5 to 6%; March: such that real wage (calculated using cost of living index for Jan.-Feb.) ≤ 12% below end-91 real wage; Quarter II-IV: such that real wage (calculated using cost of living index for previous quarter) ≤ 10% below end-91 real wage. Base changed from wage bill to average wage. Excess wage tax levied on wage increases above the guidelines excluding private enterprises and firms with less than 25 employees. Wage increases of up to 3 percentage points above limits are tax exempt, increases between 3 and 5 percentage points above limits are taxed at 200%, above 5 percentage points at	*January* Minimum wage raised to Kcs 2,200 per month. No other regulation Jan.-May due to lack of agreement in Tripartite Commission.

June Guideline increase in average wages over prorated average wages in 1991: 0% for banks + savings banks, 10% for insurance and other companies with profitability ≤ 12%, 15% for enterprises with profitability > 12%. Same tax rates as in 1991. |

Czech & Slovak Federal Republic

(continued)

1989	1990	1991	1992
		750%. Bonuses or premia from profits limited to less than 20% of the wage bill with excess of limit taxed at 750%. Minimum wage of Kcs 2,000 per month established, not indexed.	

Hungary

1989	1990	1991	1992
Continuation of tax-based incomes policy, introduced in 1988 Nominal wage increases in excess of 44% (the approximate coefficient of aggregate labour value-added) of a firm's increase of nominal value-added are non-deductible from the firm's taxable income and subject to corporate income tax. The excess wage tax does not apply to joint ventures or enterprises with revenue of less than forint 20 million.	No significant changes.	No significant changes.	*January* Abolishment of excess wage tax. *July* New Labour Code regulating labour relations similar to German labour laws. Provides for free coalition, right for trade unions to enter into collective agreements, individual negotiations between workers and employers. Firms employing more than 50 people are to establish shop councils. Trade unions may conclude collective agreements with employers if their nominees receive more than 50% of votes cast in shop council elections.

Poland

1989	1990	1991	1992

December
Each firm is subject to a wage norm equal to the wage bill in September, adjusted for 80% of meantime inflation.
Increases beyond the norm are not tax-deductible and subject to the statutory 40% corporate tax rate.

January
Indexation of the norm wage fund (on a cumulative basis) to the retail price index through a coefficient. Increases in wage funds in excess by up to 3% are subject to excess wage tax of 200%; increases above the norm between 3 and 5% are taxed at 300% and increases above the norm of more than 5% are taxed at 500%. The coefficient of indexation is set at 0.3 in January, at 0.2 in February, and at 0.6 in May. (A brief increase occurred in June at 1.0).

June
The first two rates of excess wage bill tax are reduced to 100 and 200%, respectively. The base on which tax free wage increases are computed is increased for some 10% of the labour force, adding about 2% to the norm wage fund of public enterprises as a whole.

January
Wage norm applies to a firm's average wage instead of the wage bill to prevent further excess increases in the wage in proportions to the decline in employment.
Private enterprises are exempt from the excess wage tax.
Commercialized enterprises are made subject to the tax at 80% of the rate applied to public firms, provided certain conditions are met.
Additional measures aim at stimulating adherence to the wage norm.

January
Wage norm increases by one half of the amount by which the average monthly wage in 1991 exceeded the average monthly norm in 1991.

General
Lowering of marginal excess wage increase tax rates.
Plan to forego the practice of forgiving a part of one year's violation of the wage norm starting in 1993.
Plan to shift to a system whereby the norm would no longer be indexed linked but adjusted discretely.

Romania

1989	1990	1991	1992
Wages centrally determined.	*November* Wage compensation policy in form of a flat monthly wage supplement tied to the increase in consumer prices.	*April* Excess wage tax levied on wage increases above a wage bill norm. Only enterprises with a majority of foreign ownership are tax exempted.	*January* Indexation coefficient applied to wage bill instead of individual wages.
		September Substitution of the wage compensation allowance by adjustment of individual wages using forecast inflation. Indexation coefficient set to 0.5 and adjusted periodically in consultation with trade unions dependent partly on deviation of actual from forecast inflation. Private sector tax exempted but asked to follow guidelines.	*May and September* Lump sum allowance to compensate for cut in consumer price subsidies.

Appendix III

A price equation under an excess wage increase tax

A wage determination equation, valid for the public enterprise sector during a period in which all earnings are paid out to labour, and capital is left with no return, may be written: [1]

$$(1) \qquad w_{pub} = p\left(\frac{\delta Y}{\delta L} + \frac{\delta Y}{\delta K}\frac{K}{L}\right)$$

where w_{pub} denotes the nominal wage in public enterprises, p denotes the product price, $(\delta Y/\delta L)$ and $(\delta Y/\delta K)$ denote the physical marginal product of labour and capital, respectively, and K/L is the capital-labour ratio.

Regarding wage setting in the evolving private sectors, rising unemployment due to closing or shrinking public enterprises may be assumed to cause downward pressure on the wage level. Thus, independent of the product market structure, the private sector could incur a rent during the transition period until unemployment may be assumed to have 'normalized' to a level denoted U^n.[2] The wage equation in this sector may be approximated by:

$$(2) \qquad w_{pri} = p\left(\frac{\delta Y}{\delta L} - \theta\left(U - U^n\right)\right)$$

where w_{pri} denotes the nominal wage in the private sector, θ indicates the influence of unemployment above a 'natural' level on the wage level, and U is the actual unemployment rate.

Turning to the determination of product prices, account needs to be taken of the relatively high degree of openness. Hence, even if enterprises have a monopoly or dominant market position domestically, competition from abroad could prevent its exploitation, provided the good or service is tradeable or potential competition is present. In these assumed competitive markets, firms would find it difficult to pass a tax, levied on wage increases, exceeding a certain norm, on to buyers. To simplify, for public and private enterprises operating in competitive markets, p may be assumed to be given by the international price level p^*, converted to domestic currency by multiplying with the exchange rate e (expressed in units of domestic currency per unit of foreign currency):

(3) $\quad p = p^* \, e$

Hence, for public and private enterprises who operate in markets with p assumed to be given, equations (3) and (1) on the one hand, and (3) and (2) on the other, determine the nominal wage. Public enterprises appear to be able to pay relatively higher wages, but seen from a dynamic point of view, the impact on the evolution of the firm's capital stock of such wage formation would suggest that labour and capital productivity decline. By contrast, private enterprises may experience a rising labour and capital productivity, owing to the impact of the relatively large return on capital implied by equation (2), and therefore be able to afford relatively rapid increases in wages. To the extent that the lack of servicing capital in public enterprises results in declining productivity, the wage level in these firms would have to fall.

Regarding the excess wage tax, public firms, whose management is controlled by employees, would obviously attempt to avoid the tax. Private firms in this group (if subject to the tax), who experience relatively strong productivity growth and thus could afford corresponding wage increases, have a strong incentive to avoid the regulation either, since it may hinder the morale of their work force and inhibit hiring of skilled labour.

Regarding the non-tradeables sector, high concentration suggests extraction of monopolistic rent. Firms in monopoly position may reduce output. Firms who are subsidized may pass the tax on to tax payers. Price setting by public and private enterprises operating in such markets could be approximated by mark-up pricing:

(4) $\quad p = \dfrac{w}{\dfrac{\delta Y}{\delta L}} (1-s)(1+m)\,(1 + \overset{*}{p}_m e)$

where s denotes the rate of subsidization, m denotes the profit mark-up over costs, and $p^* m$ is the import price level converted to domestic currency by multiplying with the exchange rate e. Consideration of the excess wage increase tax requires differentiating equation (4) with respect to time as below.

Regarding the wage level in private enterprises, a floor could be given by wages paid in private firms operating in competitive markets. Wages would thus be determined by equations (3) and (2). The price would then be determined by adding a profit mark-up to the given wage, reflecting the degree of extracted monopolistic rent. To the extent that these firms reinvest rent incurred, produc-

76

tivity will improve, possibly increasing rent (dependent on productivity and wage evolution in private firms operating in competitive markets). If private firms are subject to the excess wage tax, reaction appears to depend on their market power. With a strong market position, they may pass the tax on to buyers. Otherwise they may choose to avoid the tax, rather than risking a loss of market share.

Regarding public enterprises, and to the extent that these firms are labour controlled, prices would be set such that a monopolistic position tends to be fully exploited so as to accommodate wage demands. Labour does not know how a potential future owner uses the firm's assets and therefore may give little consideration to long run revenue maximization and hence the firm's market share and capital stock. The granting of subsidies and possibility of capital stock depletion facilitate accommodation of wage demands. The wage tax would obtain a minor role, because in as much as t rises, s could rise as well, with taxpayers paying the excess wage tax. Combining the price equations, using log form, and differentiating with respect to time, the inflation rate may be written:

(5) $\quad \dot{p} = \alpha(\dot{p}^* + \dot{e}) + \beta(\dot{w} - \dot{x} + \dot{m} + \dot{t} + \dot{p}_m^* + \dot{e})$

$\qquad + \gamma(\dot{w} - \dot{x} + \dot{m} + \dot{t} + \dot{p}_m + \dot{e})$

$\qquad$ *where* $\dot{t} = \dfrac{\delta t}{\delta \dot{w}} \dfrac{\delta \dot{w}}{\delta time}$, *with* $\dfrac{\delta t}{\delta \dot{w}} > 0$, *if* $\dfrac{\delta \dot{w}}{\delta time} > \dot{\overline{w}}$

$\qquad$ *where* $\dot{\overline{w}}$ *is the wage norm, and* $\dfrac{\delta t}{\delta \dot{w}}$ *dependent*

$\qquad$ *on the progressive excess wage increase tax scale,*

$\qquad$ *and with* $\alpha + \beta + \gamma = 1$

Labour productivity is denoted by x, α denotes the weight in the overall price level of price setting by private and public enterprises operating in competitive markets, β denotes the respective weight of private enterprises who have a monopolistic position, and γ is the respective weight of public enterprises in such a position. Dots above variables denote growth rates.

Notes

1 The public enterprise sectors continue to be profitable, albeit with a decreasing rate. However, as mentioned in Section 4.2., if revenue of employees tends to be maximized who have no interest in preserving the capital stock

of the enterprise, then 'profitability' could be associated with depletion of the capital stock. Equation (1) implicitly assumes, however, that the capital stock is maintained.

2 The course of unemployment, and thus this rent, would be affected by the unemployment benefit system put in place. If the system causes trade unions and workers' councils not to consider unemployment in wage bargaining, downward pressure on wages may not be present. The coefficient theta in equation (2) simply captures all influences that may account for a potential insider-outsider problem regarding the private sector.

References

Alogoskoufis, George S. (1992) 'Monetary accommodation, exchange rate regimes and inflation persistence', *Economic Journal*, vol. 102, no. 412 May, pp. 461-480.

____, and Ron Smith (1991), 'The Phillips Curve: The persistence of inflation, and the Lucas critique: evidence from exchange-rate regimes', *American Economic Review*, vol. 81, no. 5, December, pp. 1254- 1275.

____, and Alan Manning (1988), 'Unemployment persistence', *Economic Policy*, October, pp. 427-469.

Aoki, Masahiko (1988), *Information, Incentives and Bargaining in the Japanese Economy*. London.

Aukrust, O. (1970), 'Prim I: A model of the price and income distribution mechanisms of an open economy', *Review of Income and Wealth*, no. 16, pp. 51-78.

Baumol, William J. (1979), 'On some microeconomic issues in inflation theory', in Gapinski, J.H. and C.G. Rockwood (eds.), *Essays in Post-Keynesian Inflation*. Cambridge, Mass., pp. 55-78.

Benassi, Jean-Pascal (1982), *The Economics of Market Disequilibrium*, New York.

Berg, Andrew, and Olivier J. Blanchard (1992), 'Stabilization and transition: Poland 1990-91', International Monetary Fund, Seminar Series no. 1992/07, April.

Blanchard, Olivier J., (1990), 'Suggestions for a new set of fiscal indicators', Organization for Economic Cooperation and Development, *OECD Working Paper*, Paris, April.

____, and R. Layard (1990), 'Economic change in Poland', Centre for Economic Performance, Discussion Paper no. 3, London, May.

____, R. Dornbusch, M. King, P. Krugman, R. Layard, Y. Chul Park, L. Summers (1989), *World Imbalances*, Report of the World Institute for

Development Economics Research, World Economy Group, Chapter 3.

_____, and Danny Quah (1989), 'The dynamic effects of aggregate demand and supply disturbances', *American Economic Review*, vol. 79, no. 4, September, pp. 655-673.

Borensztein, Eduardo, and Peter J. Montiel (1992), 'Savings, investment, and growth in Eastern Europe', in Winckler, Georg (ed.), *Central and Eastern Europe Roads to Growth*. Papers presented at a seminar held in Baden, Austria, April 15-18, 1991. International Monetary Fund, Austrian National Bank, Washington, D.C., pp. 153-187.

_____, D.G. Demekas, and J.D. Ostry (1992), 'The output decline in the aftermath of reform: the cases of Bulgaria, Czechoslovakia, and Romania', International Monetary Fund, unpublished Working Paper, July.

Braun, Anne Romanis (1986), *Wage Determination and Incomes Policy in Open Economies*. International Monetary Fund, Washington, D.C.

Bruno, Michael (1986), 'Sharp disinflation strategy: Israel 1985', *Economic Policy*, no. 2, April, pp. 379-407.

_____ (1992), 'Stabilization and reform in Eastern Europe', *Staff Papers*, International Monetary Fund, vol. 39, no. 4, December, pp. 741-777.

Bull, Clive, and Andrew Schotter (1985), 'The Garbage Game, Inflation, and Incomes Policy', in Maital, Shlomo, and Irwin Lipnowski (eds.), *Macroeconomic Conflict and Social Institutions*, Cambridge, Mass., pp. 121-140.

Canterbery, E. Ray(1983), 'Tax reform and incomes policy: a VATIP proposal', *Journal of Post-Keynsian Economics*, vol. 5, no. 3, Spring, pp. 430-439.

Calmfors, L. and J. Driffill (1988), 'Centralization of wage bargaining and macroeconomic performance', *Economic Policy*, no. 6, pp. 13-61.

Chand, Sheetal K. (1986), 'EuropeanExperience with Tax-based Income Policies', in Colander, David C. (ed.), *Incentive-Based Incomes Policies. Advances in TIP and MAP*, Cambridge, Mass., pp. 211-230.

Csikos-Nagy, Bela (1989), 'Hungary's Living Standard Policy', in Urquidi, Victor, L. (ed.), *Incomes Policies*, Papers prepared for a Conference of the International Economic Association, New York,, pp. 233- 247.

Colander, David C. (1979), *Incomes Policies: Solutions to Inflation*, New York,.

_____ (1985), 'Why an Incomes Policy Makes an Economy More Efficient', in Maital, Shlomo, and Irwin Lipnowski (eds.), *Macroeconomic Conflict and Social Institutions*, Cambridge, Mass., pp. 97-120.

Daimond, Peter (1990), 'Comment on R. Jackman and R. Layard: The Real effects of tax-based incomes policy', *Scandinavian Journal of Economics*, vol. 92, no. 2, pp. 325-328.

Dalziel, Paul C. (1990), 'Market power, inflation, and incomes policies', *Journal of Post Keynesian Economics*, vol. 12, Spring, pp. 424-438.

Dinopoulos, Elias, and Timothy Lane (1992), 'Market liberalization policies in a reforming socialist economy', *Staff Papers*, International

Monetary Fund, vol. 39, no. 3, September, pp. 465-494.

Dooley, Michael P., and Peter Isard (1992), 'The Roles of Incentives and Planning in Market-oriented Transformations', in Richard O'Brian (ed.), *Finance and the International Economy*, vol. 6, Oxford.

Dornbusch, Rudiger, and Mario H. Simonsen (1987), *Inflation Stabilization with Incomes Policy Support*. Group of Thirty, New York and London.

Eichner, Alfred S., and J.A. Kregel (1975), 'An essay on post-Keynesian theory: a new paradigm in economics, *Journal of Economic Literature*, vol. 13, no. 4, December, pp. 1293-1314.

_____ (1983), 'Income conflicts, inflation, and controls: a response', *Journal of Post Keynesian Economics*, vol. 5, no. 4, pp. 603-607.

Elvander, Nils (1990), 'Incomes policies in the Nordic countries', *International Labor Review*, vol. 129, no. 1, pp. 1-21.

Eucken, Walter (1952), *Grundsaetze der Wirtschaftspolitik*. Bern and Tuebingen.

Flanagan, Robert J., David W. Soskice, and Lloyd Ulman (1983), *Unionism, Economic Stabilization, and Incomes Policies: European Experience*. The Brookings Institution, Washington, D.C.

Galbraith, James K. (1952), *A Theory of Price Controls*. Cambridge, Mass.

Giavazzi, Francesco, and Marco Pagano (1990), 'Can severe fiscal contractions be expansionary? Tales of two small european countries.' National Bureau of Economic Research, *NBER Working Paper*, no. 3372, May.

Guidotti, Pablo, E., and Carlos A. Vegh (1991), 'The optimal inflation tax when money reduces transaction costs: a reconsideration', International Monetary Fund, Mimeographed.

Haberler, Gottfried (1971), *Incomes Policies and Inflation. An Analysis of Basic Principles. With a Prologue on the New Economic Policy of August 1971*, American Enterprise Institute, Washington, D.C.

_____ (1982), 'Inflation and incomes policy', *Economic Notes. Monte Dei Paschi di Siena*, no. 2, pp. 20-46.

von Hayek, Friedrich A. (1948), *Individualism and Economic Order*. The University of Chicago, Chicago.

Hemming, Richard (1992), 'Privatization of State Enterprises', in Tanzi, Vito, (ed.), *Fiscal Policies in Economies in Transition*. International Monetary Fund, Washington, D.C., pp. 80-100.

Henry, S.G.B., and Omerod, P. (1979), 'Rational expectations in a wage-price model of the U.K.', Paper presented to SSRC conference on Rational Expectations, University of Sussex.

Hinds, Manuel (1991), 'Issues in the Introduction of Market Forces in Eastern European Socialist Economies', in Commander, Simon (ed.), *Managing Inflation in Socialist Economies in Transition*. The World Bank, Washington, pp. 121-154.

Husain, Aasim, M. (1992), 'Private sector development in state-dominated economies', International Monetary Fund, unpublished Working Paper

Husain, Aasim, M. and Ratna Sahay (1992), 'Does sequencing of privatization matter in reforming planned economies?' *Staff Papers*, vol. 39, no. 4, International Monetary Fund, December, pp. 801-824.

Jackman, R., and Richard Layard (1990), 'The real effects of taxed-based incomes policies', *Scandinavian Journal of Economics*, vol. 92, Nr. 2, pp. 309-324.

_____, _____, and Steven Nickell (1991), *Unemployment, Macroeconomic Performance and the Labour Market*, London.

Johnson, Harry G., (1972) 'Notes on Incomes Policy and the Balance of Payments', in Parkin, Michael and Michael T. Sumner (eds.) *Incomes Policy and Inflation*, Manchester, pp. 268-278.

Koford, Kenneth J., and Jeffrey B. Miller (1986), 'Incentive Anti-inflation Policies in a Model of Market Disequilibrium', in Colander, David C. (ed.), *Incentive-Based Incomes Policies. Advances in TIP and MAP*, Cambridge, Mass., pp. 71-93.

Kydland, F. and E.C. Prescott (1977), 'Rules rather than discretion: the inconsistency of optimal plans', *Journal of Political Economy*, vol. 85, pp. 473-492.

Lane, Timothy, and Elias Dinopoulos (1991), 'Fiscal constraints on market-oriented reform in a socialist economy', International Monetary Fund, unpublished Working Paper, August.

_____ (1992), 'Household demand for money in Poland', *Staff Papers*, International Monetary Fund, vol. 39, no. 4, December, pp. 825-854.

_____ (1991), 'Wage controls and employment in a socialist economy', International Monetary Fund, unpublished Working Paper, November.

Layard, Richard, (1991) 'Issues in the Introduction of Market Forces in Eastern European Socialist Economies', in Commander, Simon (ed.), *Managing Inflation in Socialist Economies in Transition*, The World Bank, Washington, pp. 213-246.

_____ (1990), 'Wage bargaining and incomes policy: possible lessons for Eastern Europe.' Discussion Paper no. 2, Centre for Economic Performance. London School for Economics and Political Science, London.

_____ (1986), *How to Beat Unemployment*, New York.

_____ (1982), 'Is incomes policy the answer to unemployment?', *Economica*, vol. 49, Nr. 195, August, pp. 219-239.

Lerner, Abba, P., and David C. Colander (1980), *MAP: A Market Anti-Inflation Plan*, New York,.

Lewis, Philip E.T., and Michael G. Kirby (1988), 'A new approach to modelling the effects of incomes policies', *Economics Letters*, vol. 28, no. 2, pp. 81-85.

Lipnowski, Irwin, and Shlomo Maital (1985), 'Hanging Together or Separately: A Game-theoretic Approach to Macroeconomic Conflict', in Shlomo Maital and Irwin Lipnowski (eds.), *Macroeconomic Conflict and Social Institutions*, Cambridge, Mass., pp. 39-96.

82

Lipton, David, and Jeffrey Sachs (1990), 'Creating a market economy in Eastern Europe: the case of Poland', *Brookings Papers on Economic Activity*, no. 1, pp. 75-147.

Malinvaud, Edmond (1990), 'The macroeconomic tradeoffs of price and income policies', *Scandinavian Journal of Economics*, vol. 92, no. 2, pp. 331-343.

Moene, Karl O. (1990), 'Comment on R. Jackman and R. Layard: The real effects of tax-based incomes policy', *Scandinavian Journal of Economics*, vol. 92, no. 2, pp. 329-330.

Milesi-Ferretti, Gian Maria (1992), 'Wage claims, incomes policy, and the path of output and inflation in a formerly centrally planned economy', International Monetary Fund, Washington, unpublished Working Paper, September.

Okun, Arthur M. (1981), *Prices and Quantities: A Macroeconomic Analysis*, Brookings Institution, Washington, D.C.,.

Paci, Pierella (1988), 'Tax-based incomes policies: will they work? have they worked?', *Fiscal Studies*, vol. 9, no. 2, May, pp. 81-94.

Pencavel, John H. (1981), 'The American Experience with Incomes Policies', in Fallick, J. L., and R.F. Elliott (eds.), *Incomes Policies, Inflation and Relative Pay*, London, pp. 155-186.

Rakowski, James J. (1983), 'Income conflicts, inflation and controls', *Journal of Post Keynesian Economics*, vol. 5, no. 4, pp. 590-602.

Sachs, Jeffrey D., (1983) 'Real wages and unemployment in the OECD countries', *Brookings Papers on Economic Activity*, no. 1, pp. 255-289.

Sargan, D. J. (1980), 'A model of wage-price inflation', *Review of Economic Studies*, vol. 47, no. 1, pp. 97-112.

Seidman, Laurence S. (1978), 'Tax-based incomes policies', *Brookings Papers on Economic Activity*, vol. 2, pp. 301-348.

Schaffer, Mark E. (1992), 'The polish state-owned enterprise sector and the recession of 1990', *Comparative Economic Studies*, vol. 34, Spring, pp. 58-85.

Sumner, Michael T., and Robert A. Jones (1972), 'A Survey of the Econometric Evidence of the Effects of Incomes Policy on the Rate of Inflation', in Parkin, Michael, and Michael T. Summer (eds.), *Incomes Policy and Inflation*, Manchester, pp. 1-29.

Tobin, James (1984), 'The case for incomes policies', *Challenge*, A Symposium: Incomes Policy, March/April, pp. 52-57; reprinted in James Tobin (Jackson, P.M. (ed.)) (1987a), *Policies for Prosperity. Essays in a Keynesian Mode*, Cambridge, Mass., pp. 375-379.

_____ (1986), Forewordin David Colander (ed.), *Incentive-Based Incomes Policies: Advances in TIP and MAP*, Ballinger, Cambridge, Mass., pp. xvii-xv; reprinted in James Tobin (Jackson, P.M. (ed.)) (1987b), *Policies for Prosperity. Essays in a Keynesian Mode*, Cambridge, Mass., pp. 382-385.

_____ (1980), 'Stabilization policy ten years after', *Brookings Papers on Economic*

Activity', no. 1, pp. 19-71.

Turnovsky, Stephen J., and John D. Pitchford (1978), 'Expectations and Income Claims in Wage Price Determination: An Aspect of the Inflationary Process', Chapter 10 in Bergstrom, Albert R. et. al. (eds.), *Stability and Inflation*, Chichester, pp. 155-178.

Wallich, Henry C., and Sidney Weintraub (1971), 'A tax-based incomes policy', *Journal of Economic Issues*, vol. V., no. 4, September, pp. 1-19.

Wallis, K. (1980), 'Econometric implications of the rational expectations hypothesis', *Econometrica*, vol. 48, no. 1, pp. 49-73.

Weintraub, Sidney (1972), 'Incomes policy: completing the stabilization triangle', *Journal of Economic Issues*, vol. 6, no. 4, December, pp. 105-122.

Whitley, J. D. (1986), 'A model of incomes policy in the U.K. 1963-79', *Manchester School of Economics and Social Studies*, vol. 54, March, pp. 31-64.

Williamson, John, (ed.) (1985) *Inflation and Indexation. Argentina, Brazil, and Israel*, Institute for International Economics, Washington.

Part Two
ASPECTS OF TRANSITION

1 Introduction

Eastern European countries are in their fifth year of transition to market economies. Major successes of the stabilization and restructuring programs, adopted by the six countries Bulgaria, the Czech and Slovak Republics, the Republic of Hungary, the Republic of Poland, and Romania, have been nearly complete price liberalization associated with elimination of substantial monetary overhangs in Bulgaria, Poland and Romania, strong export performance in all countries and, owing to rising private savings, generally improving external current account balances despite increasing fiscal deficits, a turn towards privatization in earnest in Bulgaria, Poland and Romania following a period of hesitation, and thus a tackling of the 'corporate governance' problem which lies at the heart of successful transformation, establishment of exchange and trade systems providing for relatively unrestricted external trade and hence strengthened domestic competition, and establishment of social safety nets to protect both relatively large portions of the populations that are not part of the labour force and the unemployed. Further achievements are introduction of bankruptcy laws and improvements of the legal systems, planned and partly implemented modern tax systems that aim at minimizing distortions while providing for strong incentives to work, invest and save, establishment of both central banks who will control the money supply through indirect means and banking systems of the universal type. In accordance with theoretical reasoning, opinion polls indicate that in the Czech Republic, Hungary and Poland elimination of the characteristics of a shortage economy appears to have resulted in little declining or rising living standards during the three years period of stabilization and restructuring, despite the substantial measured cumulative output and real wage declines. Given these accomplishments and indications for growth to have resumed in some of the considered countries and its likelihood to resume in the near future in the remaining countries, it appears warranted to emphasize continuation of tight macroeconomic policy so as to not permit flow problems to undermine what has been achieved and what could be achieved in the medium term. The generally high unemployment rates, the relatively large spreads between lending and deposit interest rates, and volatility of real interest rates cannot be seen in isolation of these flow problems as given, foremost, by generally relatively high fiscal deficits, but they warrant an own analysis which, together with an examination of the flow problem, is the purpose of this paper. The paper takes a forward-looking approach, based on a medium- and long-term view,[1] but it does so in considering conditions set by Eastern European societies for an economic order, as expressed, for instance, in the adopted labour laws and tax systems. It is organized as follows: Section 2 addresses the unemployment problem considering, in particular, that unemployment could become persistent, Section 3 examines the evolution of financial systems with particular regard to requirements for efficient capital allocation, and Section 4 discusses the presumable cause for a continuation of relatively high inflation, fiscal deficits. Section 5 summarizes and contains concluding remarks.

Notes

1   It may be noted that, with regard to industrial countries, the hypothesis of a 'political business cycle' has not found support in empirical analyses.

2 The unemployment problem

1. Introduction

Analysis of unemployment is complex and can take many routes. Regarding industrial countries, it is contested, in some circles, whether it represents an analytically meaningful concept and a serious social problem. Regarding Eastern European countries, open unemployment has been a new experience and could contribute to instability of the market economies and political systems. At the outset it may be stated that only long term involuntary unemployment reveals deficiencies of a market economy, because continuous structural change in a world of imperfect markets implies friction. Given the extent to which production structures in Eastern European countries have to adjust, temporary unemployment regarding areas of particular skills may appear unavoidable. However, the transition to market economies has raised unemployment in some Eastern European countries to double digit levels which could become persistent. Hence the goal should be for present unemployment rates not to result in long term involuntary unemployment or, perhaps equally important, labour force withdrawal. This Section briefly describes, first, developments pertaining to Eastern European labour markets, utilizes then the major approaches offered by economic theory in an attempt to evaluate unemployment in Eastern Europe, considers subsequently the major findings of the industrial relations literature regarding productivity growth and participation of labour in firms' decision making, and finally draws conclusions with respect to labour market policies in Eastern Europe.

2. Recent labour market developments

The evolution of unemployment among Eastern European countries differs

Table 2.1
Czech and Slovak Republics: rate of unemployment 1991-92

(As per cent of the Labour Force)

| | 1991 | | | | 1992 | | | |
	March	June	Sep	Dec	Mar	June	Sept	Dec*
Czech Republic	1.7	2.6	3.8	4.1	3.7	2.7	2.6	2.4
Slovak Republic	3.7	6.3	9.6	11.8	12.3	11.3	10.6	10.1

Source: International Monetary Fund, Data Fund.

* Preliminary.

markedly. Starting from a situation of chronic excess demand for labour prior to the adoption of macroeconomic reform and structural adjustment programs in 1990,[1] open unemployment rose rapidly during 1991 in all countries, except in Romania (Fig. 2.1).[2] In the course of 1992 it reached double digit levels in Bulgaria, Hungary, Poland and the Slovak Republic. In Romania it climbed to about 9 per cent but is estimated to have further risen in the course of 1993. The unemployment rates in Bulgaria and Hungary appear to stabilize in 1993.[3] In Poland, the trend of unemployment shows a slight increase. By contrast, in the Czech and Slovak Republics the trend is decreasing since early and mid-1992, respectively. Unemployment in the Czech Republic rose to merely 4.1 per cent at the end of 1991 before full or near full employment was restored in the second half of 1992.[4] The question thus arises as to the factors that explain the fundamentally different evolution of unemployment in the Czech and Slovak Republics, on the one hand, and in the remaining countries, on the other. By itself, such an examination may suggest solutions. It ought to be noted, however, that the extent of long run involuntary unemployment is not clear. This knowledge would facilitate an assessment regarding factors that may prevent adjustment to full employment. In addition, since labour is not homogenous, ideally, the major segments of the labour market would need to be identified so as to derive solutions for each of those where long term unemployment is present. However, given the above summarized characteristics, it appears not too restrictive to assume that mainly less skilled labour is affected, because the restructuring of both public enterprises and the institutional infrastructure with given rapid growth of private economic activity creates demand for skilled labour which probably cannot be satisfied. To the extent that long term unemployment of less skilled labour persists, differences to the unemployment problem in industrial countries could prove to be not very marked, which would permit utilization of the extensive theoretical and empirical analysis regarding unemployment in these countries.

The divergent evolution of unemployment raises two questions: what may explain the decreasing unemployment trends in the Czech and Slovak Republics

90

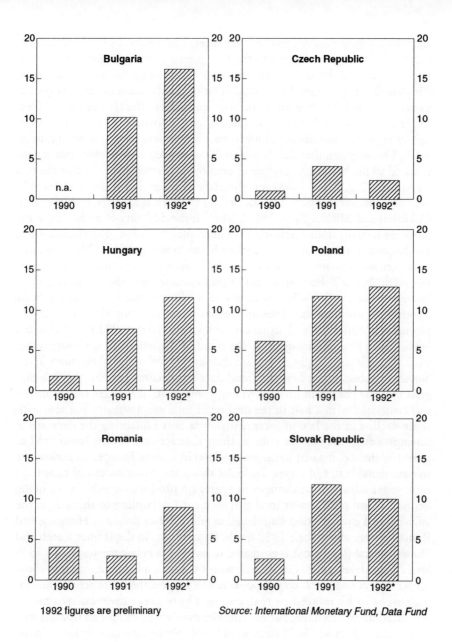

Figure 2.1 Selected Eastern European countries: unemployment
(as per cent of the labour force; end of period)

91

and why are their unemployment levels lower than the average? Table 2.1 shows that the trend became negative in the first quarter of 1992 regarding the Czech Republic, and in the second quarter of 1992 regarding the Slovak Republic. This break was preceded by a curtailment of the duration of unemployment benefits from 12 to 6 months in both countries effective January 1992. Eligibility for social benefits available after the six months period is rather tightly regulated and the social subsistence allowances appear to be of modest form. This suggests, that the change in the unemployment benefit system contributed to the halt in the decline of employment since early 1992 in the two Republics (Fig. 2.2).[5] However, the view of a simple inverse relationship between income support and incentives to work is an oversimplification (Atkinson and Micklewright, 1991). There is the difficulty of measuring accurately movements from employment to unemployment, out of the labour force, and backward movements. The decline in unemployment could be associated with either, labour force withdrawal and/or a flow into uncompensated unemployment. Fig. 2.2 shows some fall of the labour force in the Czech Republic. Positive population growth associated with a falling labour force could indicate labour force withdrawals.[6] If the difference (in terms of people) between unemployment at end-1991 and actual unemployment during 1992 is added to the labour force figures during 1992, the trend of the latter still decreases somewhat. There is also a slight downward shift in the level of the labour force in the Slovak Republic, albeit here the trend does not decline. In sum, Fig. 2.2 suggests that the change in unemployment compensation in these two countries was associated with a halt in the decline of total employment, but also with some decline in the labour force. Further factors explaining the decrease in unemployment may be the same as those that account for the lower level of unemployment compared to the average level in Eastern Europe. To explore the role attributable to real wages, Table 2.2 shows the evolution of real consumption wages adjusted for changes in aggregate productivity, the latter being defined as real output over total employment.[7] According to these data, the adjusted real consumption wage levels at end 1992 in Bulgaria, Hungary, and Romania were above their 1989 levels. By contrast, in the former Czech and Slovak Federal Republic it is estimated to have been below the respective 1989 level. Wage developments in Poland, where the unemployment rate rose above 13 per cent at end 1992, could appear not to support the hypothesis for unemployment to be related to real wages. There are, however, two major qualifications in this respect whose consideration would call for an upward revision of the indices which, in turn, would probably be substantially larger in the case of Poland than for the other countries. First, if the indices are interpreted as pertaining to public sector wage developments, an adjustment would be required to account for a potential divergence of productivity in the private and public sector. At the outset of transition, Poland's private sector share in GDP (about 30 per cent) was substantially larger and since then private sector eco-

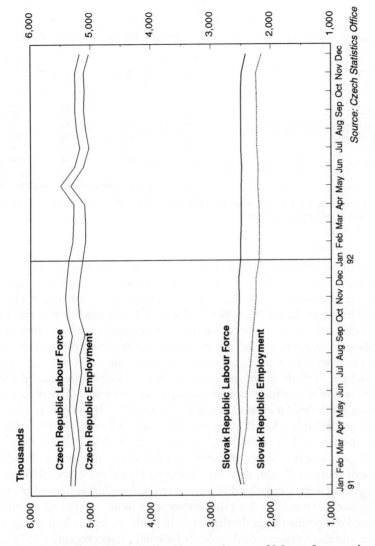

Figure 2.2 Czech and Slovak Republics: evolution of labour force and employment 1991-92

nomic growth stronger as compared to the other countries with the share reaching about 45 per cent at end 1992. Hence, under the assumption that productivity did not fall in the private sector, the decrease in adjusted real wages shown in Table 2.2 for Poland's public sector would be substantially overestimated and, under the assumption for productivity to have evolved evenly in private sectors of Eastern European economies, this overestimation would

Table 2.2
Selected Eastern European countries:
indices of real consumption wages adjusted for aggregate productivity [a]

	1989	1990	1991	1992 [b]
		(rounded)		
Bulgaria	100	110	89	105
Czech & Slovak Federal Republic	100	101	84	98
Hungary	100	104	115	129
Poland	100	76	81	75
Romania	100	117	116	105

Source: International Monetary Fund, Data Fund.

a Real consumption wages and productivity figures are end of period estimates. The latter are based on ratios of real output to total employment.
b Preliminary.

exceed that which would pertain to public sectors in the other countries. In fact, the figures shown for Poland would become rather meaningless. (Analogous, increases of adjusted real wages in public sectors, as, for instance, in Hungary, would be larger than those shown in Table 2.2). A second downwards bias of the indices is given by the following fact: if firms may be assumed, for a moment, to be profit maximizers, then what matters for employment is the real product wage. Since producer prices rose generally by less than consumer prices,[8] the declines in adjusted real wages would be overestimated and the increases underestimated from an employer's point of view. The adverse terms of trade shock that hit Poland's economy during 1990-91 (24 per cent) has been substantially larger than the one that affected the former Czech and Slovak Republic (about 17 per cent) and Hungary (about 10 per cent), suggesting, *ceteris paribus*, that the figures shown in Table 2.2 would need to be adjusted upwards more for Poland than for the former Czech and Slovak Republic and Hungary. In sum, there would be two reasons calling for an upward revision of the indices presented in the Table if they were to be interpreted as reflecting adjusted real product wage developments in public sectors including state enterprises, and this revision would probably have to be larger regarding Poland than with respect to the other countries. Real wage developments could therefore provide an important explanatory factor for the evolution of unemployment and its divergence among Eastern European countries. However, given that firms have been largely labour controlled, cost pressure may not be regarded as a valid argument in explaining unemployment. A response to this objection may be seen in the lag between rising cost pressure and the firm's employment decision. Even if a firm is not servicing capital and possibly depleting its capital stock, employment cannot be held constant for long. The improvement of incentives to privatize, 'hardening' of state-firms budget constraints through introduction of bankruptcy laws, cuts in subsidies, and credit restraint, made it even more difficult for public enterprises to maintain employment levels in the face of real wages declining by less than productivity.

Understanding of the divergence of employment levels in Eastern Europe may require to consider the macroeconomic context. Together with Hungary, the former Czech and Slovak Federal Republic entered the transition period without having to eliminate a substantial monetary overhang. In connection with less large fiscal deficits than average during the 1990-92 period, this meant substantially less inflation than average and an external current account slightly in surplus. Given the experience gained from stabilization and structural adjustment attempts internationally during the past decade, it is clear that market participants' expectations, which determine investment and savings behaviour, money demand, and capital flows, can only be affected as intended if adjustment of the macroeconomic 'fundamentals,' (i.e., the fiscal balance, the balance of payments, and the aggregate real wage level), is evaluated in the average opinion of market participants as credible and sufficient to be sustainable. Granting the central bank relative independence, providing for strong incentives to privatize, introducing labour laws and an unemployment compensation system that promote labour mobility and search activity on the part of unemployed and employers, promoting exit of firms that are not economically viable in the long run under market conditions, contributes to a favourable assessment by markets of fundamentals. The former Czech and Slovak Federal Republic has been relatively quick in implementing these measures.[9] In addition, the Czech and Slovak Republics enjoy comparatively low external debt burdens as a result of which the share in export receipts used up to service external debt has been relatively low and declined continuously to 13 per cent in 1992 in the former unified Republic. This facilitated imports of capital goods and contributed to maintaining the highest average annual share of gross fixed capital formation in GDP in Eastern Europe during the initial stabilization phase 1990-91 (24 per cent).[10] It thus appears that the macroeconomic environment, owing to conservative demand management policies pursued before and during transition, has been more favourable in the Czech and Slovak Republics than in any other of the considered Eastern European countries which, together with both an evolution of the aggregate real wage level approximately aligned with productivity growth and the change of the unemployment compensation system, may largely explain why the employment levels were higher and decreased in contrast to the remainder of the considered Eastern European economies.

Turning to other recent labour market developments, labour laws have been introduced or were revised. The former Czech and Slovak Federal Republic took the lead in reforming these laws when a labour code was introduced in March 1991. Hungary followed in July 1992. Poland's situation has been different because the leading trade union influenced labour market regulations several years prior to transition and thus Poland had the most modern labour code in centrally-planned economies, which was revised in mid-1992 and awaits still further revision. Labour codes in Bulgaria and Romania are awaiting revision. The new labour laws in the Czech and Slovak Republics, Hungary, and Poland do not appear to unduly restrict employers' freedom of action regarding hiring and labour shedding, which may be judged to be the central feature of labour codes as regards their effect on labour mobility, structural change and thus on growth and employment. Specifically, the laws adopted by the Czech and Slovak Republics permit lay-offs of persons hired for a definite period without notice under certain circumstances. In Hungary, the lay-off period ranges from 30 to 60 days, dependent on the length of employment in the firm, and in Poland it extends to a maximum of 90 days. All four countries adopted rules of labour participation in decision-making of firms, particularly in large ones and stock-holding companies. While the potential economic effects of such participation are briefly reviewed in Section 4 below, the economic implication of fairly flexible rules regarding dismissals is that unemployment may not be attributable to employers being deterred from hiring due to relatively high shadow costs of firing restrictions.

Measures were implemented or are planned that aim at improving market transparency, training, search activity, and labour mobility. To improve labour market transparency several countries established regional labour centres and labour exchanges. Training incentives and incentives to increase search activity were institutionalized in Hungary, where a National Training Council was established in early 1991. Similar arrangements have been made or are in the process of being implemented in all other Eastern European countries. However, an incentive problem emerged: the differential between income support during retraining and unemployment benefits has been relatively narrow which may explain, to some extent, very limited or declining attendance. All countries aim at improved vocational training, given that unemployment rates are higher among workers with this education than among less skilled people and that young people are particularly affected.

A further important development regarding labour markets are programs adopted in all Eastern European countries providing for subsidization of housing mainly by means of loans. Given the negligence of this part of the physical capital stock under central planning, externalities corroborate this decision: without available housing, labour mobility is limited contributing to inefficiencies and unemployment. Even if real wages were flexible, unemployment could not decline rapidly when labour is not mobile. Therefore, under present circumstances, unavailability of housing may be viewed as constituting the case of an adverse externality if unemployment may be attributable to labour not being sufficiently mobile due to past distortions inflicted on the housing market. However, in a market economy, the granting of subsidies should be based on knowledge of presence of an externality and periodically reviewed.

96

Finally, a key feature of any labour market is given by the adopted wage bargaining system. The unemployment experience in industrial countries taught that a system of centralized wage bargaining appears to be a key factor in explaining low unemployment (Calmfors and Driffill, 1988; Layard, 1990). Centralized bargaining facilitates alignment of wage growth and productivity growth in the aggregate, because it promotes understanding of the fact that raising wages relative to the price level contributes to unemployment. A real wage level exceeding the feasible one may thus be prevented.[11] During the initial stabilization phase, when methods of privatization, particularly regarding large enterprises, where uncertain and hence it was not clear whether managements of state enterprises would maximize profits and service capital, the considered Eastern European countries pursued incomes policies in the form of wage indexation and progressive taxes levied on wage increases exceeding a certain norm to promote wage adjustment.[12] Negotiations concerning these policies where carried out within the institutional set-up of a 'Tripartite Commission' (Bulgaria, the Czech and Slovak Republics, and recently established in Poland) or 'National Interest Coordination Council' (Hungary) comprising the government, employers and trade unions, or with trade unions (Romania). It appears, however, that, in general, private employers have not yet been well organized. Regarding industrial countries, a precondition for centralized wage bargaining to be able to result in aligned growth of wages and productivity proved to be the degree of coordination among both employers' federations and trade unions. Thus, the question arises as to whether organization of employers' federations can be promoted and whether the future wage bargaining systems that evolve from the presently generally centralized wage negotiations will remain so or become industry or firm level bargaining systems.

3. Economic theory

Before proceeding to a brief review of the major approaches economic theory offers to explaining unemployment and utilizing them subsequently in an attempt to analyse unemployment in Eastern Europe, empirical observations may be noted so as to remove one potential misconception. Given two hundred years of history of industrial development, it appears that technological progress, the capital stock, and the labour force do not adversely affect the employment level, at least not in the long run (Layard and Nickel, 1985). If there exists involuntary unemployment, a society has the option to engineer substitution of labour for capital and thus bring about full employment through a change of their relative price, i.e. by permitting the price of labour (real product wage including social security contributions and pensions) to decrease relative to that of capital (real interest rate). If real wage flexibility cannot be improved, then a sustainable rise of the employment level can be accomplished only through a rise of productivity, which implies improvements of labour and/or capital and/or an increase in the capital labour ratio. Regarding Eastern Europe, it may not be controversial for a permanent increase in the capital labour ratio to be the most efficient means to raise the employment level.[13]

Seven major theoretical approaches are to be distinguished that explain unemployment, the latter four having been conceived of in response to the difficulty to interpret Western European high unemployment levels as being the result of rising 'natural' rates. Consideration of these latter theories may be justified as follows: unemployment in Eastern Europe was initially caused by the decision to transform the economies and exacerbated owing to external shocks. Hence, a policy dilemma is perceived, given by an apparent impossibility to simultaneously achieve closure of public enterprises which could not sustain market pressure, provision of training and incomes support to unemployed, promotion of private economic activity, and, ideally, fiscal surpluses. Theoretically, however, the hypothesis of impossibility may not hold. Actual developments may corroborate theory.[14] Therefore, unemployment, if persistent, could be the result of insufficient adjustment and the macroeconomic imbalances faced by Eastern Europe would then, in principle, not be different from those in several industrialized countries, particularly in Western Europe. Thus, consideration of these unemployment theories may prove rewarding if a long term view is taken and if the potential for persistence is considered.

According to the view that macroeconomic fluctuations result from dynamic optimizing behaviour by economic agents who face no quantity constraints (new classical macroeconomics), unemployment would be entirely voluntary, being the result of intertemporal substitution between consumption and leisure.[15] In this model observed unemployment is the result of agents optimizing the trade-off between consumption and leisure through time. Although it has been decisively rejected empirically[16] and its ability in explaining unemployment hysteresis is very limited, caution appears warranted in dismissing it: time preferences as to consumption and leisure differ among economic agents. Each individual faces a subjective reservation wage and discount rate which he/she applies to future earnings and consumption. With a given social security system, the larger both the reservation wage and discount rate, the higher, *ceteris paribus*, tends unemployment to be. This underlines the significance of the unemployment compensation system as one aspect of the institutional side affecting unemployment. Assessment of this institutional side provides a second approach in the analysis. A narrow institutional one would concentrate on regulations concerning wage bargaining, trade unions, labour-management relations (industrial relations system), lay offs, the unemployment benefit system, training arrangements and other incentives to increase search activity on the part of both unemployed and employers, strike activity, and labour market transparency to reduce market imperfections. This approach would also include an analysis of remaining regulations that still reduce mobility of factors of production and conserve allocative inefficiencies. A third approach would be given by the traditional analysis of the potential contribution of the real wage level to unemployment stemming from the distinction between Keynesian and classical unemployment. A fourth approach would concentrate on the slope of the demand for and supply of labour schedules and thus attempt to infer whether the curves, which may possibly be inversely sloped, intersect at a narrow angle so that the tendency towards equilibrium following a disturbance may be weak. A fifth approach may be given by the efficiency wage theory. Sixth, the insider-outsider theory could be applicable. Seventh, Solow (1990) emphasized an institutional aspect of the labour market: since the labour market is a market not for goods but for people it may be largely norm guided such that unemployed do not engage in wage cutting competition. This may be an equilibrium strategy for workers and firms: unemployed take chances to be employed at the going wage some time in the future rather than offering to work at a lower wage, because the latter may invoke competition on the labour market to a degree (in the Hobbesian sense) nobody accepts. Since nobody offers to undercut the wage, firms cannot lower them. Society accepts unemployment because it believes that reducing it would require an unacceptable degree of competition.

Based on these approaches, the following assessment of the evolving unemployment problem in Eastern European countries attempts to derive policy implications which are summarized in Section 5 below.

The intertemporal substitution theory may be regarded as having limited power in contributing to a theoretical solution of the unemployment problem in Eastern Europe, because it would suggest for unemployment to be voluntary. However, it points to the social security system as one factor that may contribute to unemployment and the reforms and curtailments of unemployment compensation in Eastern Europe indicate that the authorities implicitly acted according to it. The experience of declining unemployment in the Czech and Slovak Republics following the change of the compensation system broadens the existing empirical evidence for industrial countries on this question. Turning to other aspects of the institutional side, it has been mentioned that the adopted wage bargaining systems appear crucial. The evolution of real wages in the Czech and Slovak Republics in line with the productivity decline may be viewed as a result primarily of cooperation achieved in the employed tripartite commission. Political factors may explain why adjustment in the other Eastern European countries, who also employ such commissions, appears to have been less successful. By international comparison, the introduced labour laws may not be regarded as overly restrictive from an employer's point of view. The potential impact of the industrial relations system, including labour-management relations, is discussed in the following section. As mentioned above, training incentives and institutions promoting search activity were introduced or are planned in all

Eastern European countries as well as measures to improve labour market transparency.

Regarding allocational inefficiencies, the price systems have been nearly entirely liberalized, but privatization of particularly large enterprises proved difficult in all countries. Introduction of 'hard budget constraints' (i.e. elimination of subsidies, strengthening of credit constraints, threat of bankruptcy)[17] did not result in a widespread liquidation of these entities: persistence of the inter-enterprise arrears problem on the part of public enterprises in some countries could suggest that banks view the economic costs of forcing borrowers into bankruptcy as too high. The behaviour of the borrower will, in turn, be affected, because he considers this fact. To the extent that the latter occurs, a hidden but powerful barrier to efficient resource allocation may be given by 'soft' loans provided in order to protect loan portfolios of banks which could be regarded as one factor contributing to generally large spreads between lending and deposit interest rates as evaluated in Section 3.4. Government subsidies including those to traditional branches of production such as mining (particularly coal) and heavy industries (particularly steel) are reduced and will possibly be eliminated.[18] Remaining subsidies to public enterprises concern those commonly granted in industrial countries (public transportation, education, culture etc.). Housing is generally subsidized through loan programs, which may appear justified if these subsidies have only one aim, namely to improve labour mobility without creating new distortions and thus they should not affect the urban centres where unemployment is low. An additional barrier may be seen in tariffs which are relatively high in the case of agricultural goods.[19] Regarding the fundamental question as to whether unemployment could be reduced by delaying adjustment, the following basic arguments may be considered. Without adjustment, uncertainty regarding the evolution of the fiscal balance appears greater than under termination of direct or indirect loss coverage of public enterprises, because the burden posed by the resulting increase in unemployment under the latter case and the needed retraining measures may be ascertainable (albeit with a significant margin of error)[20] whereas the future burden posed by a continuation of subsidization would not be measurable, particularly if indirect adverse effects on growth are considered. This uncertainty influences the evaluation of government policies by domestic and foreign market participants and thus their savings, investment, and consumption behaviour. With a rise in uncertainty, time horizons may shorten and socially beneficial domestic investments may be crowded out by less beneficial ones. The assets of liquidated public enterprises would not be lost. Private investors or managements and employees of public enterprises would acquire and combine them to provide goods and services in accordance with the comparative advantages of the economy. Besides their potential to cause a shortening of time horizons, rising fiscal deficits are likely to crowd out private investment and to adversely affect inflationary expectations with an impact on interest rates and capital flows (see Section 4, below). Financing of fiscal deficits through external borrowing could alleviate the effects on domestic interest rates, but this would leave market participants uncertain as to future taxation and inflation and the resulting higher external debt servicing burden may directly adversely affect capital formation and indirectly through reduced capital inflows and inflationary expectations. In addition, given the implemented curtailments of unemployment compensation, a rise in unemployment will tend to contain wage inflation and thus promote growth of private sectors and enhance external competitiveness. Temporary rising unemployment concomitant with an improvement of the fiscal balances could therefore be regarded as promoting the transformation process, growth and employment.

Turning to the relationship between real wages and unemployment, the extensive analysis regarding the distinction between classical and Keynesian unemployment in industrial countries proved fruitless. However, the importance of both the real wage level and its flexibility is not controversial. Evidence for OECD countries shows that the latter can explain about seventy per cent of the variation in the change of unemployment from the early 1970s to the early 1980s (Layard, Nickel, Jackman, 1991, Table 3, p. 409).[21] Real wage flexibility in Japan appears to contribute substantially to the high employment level.[22] Sachs (1983) showed that the general rise in unemployment in Western Europe, following the oil shocks in the 1970s, was related to a divergence between real wages and productivity and thus to the real wage level.[23] Moreover, according to regression results (for the period 1955-86) for 16 OECD countries, the hypothesis for increases in the wedge between the real product wage and the real consumption wage (taxes on wages, indirect taxes, and import prices relative to producer prices) to raise the real product wage in the long run cannot be rejected at conventional significance levels (OECD, 1990, p. 174). Although it would be difficult to explain how such increases can be borne by capital in the long run, this finding points to the potential importance of changes in taxes that affect the wage wedge and thus labour demand. The implication would be that these taxes or external adverse shocks have the potential to depress labour demand for a considerable period. The study also finds that the hypothesis for a switch of a given tax burden from employee to employer to be incident in the long run upon the employer cannot be rejected either. Therefore, tax policies could have even long run effects on the real product wage and influence employment. Owing to the unavailability of real product wages for some Eastern European countries, Table 2.2 compared the evolution of real consumption wage indices which are less powerful in analysing unemployment. However, as discussed above, under certain assumptions, the divergence of unemployment levels in Eastern European countries appears to be related to the evolution of real wages and given the cited evidence for OECD countries, the conclusion may be drawn for real product wage levels and their flexibility to be a crucial factor in determining employment growth.[24]

As already noted, the analytical approaches advanced to explain unemployment hysteresis may contribute to a theoretical solution of the unemployment problem in Eastern Europe. There are four major concepts.[25] The demand for and supply of labour schedules could be inversely sloped and intersect at a narrow angle, giving rise to fragile equilibria and thus a weak tendency towards equilibrium following a disturbance (Blanchard and Summers, 1988). As regards supply of labour in Eastern Europe, the assumption for it to be a positive function of the real wage does not appear unreasonable. Given the experience of relatively high inflation during the transition period, money illusion may not be present. Supply could be rather elastic, because relatively large portions of the populations are presently not part of the labour force and hence a rise of the real wage may induce them to join the labour force. In addition, presently high unemployment could cause withdrawals from the labour force owing to discouragement. With rising employment these workers may be encouraged to re-enter the labour force and hence labour supply may increase. Thus, it may be reasonable to view labour supply as a function of primarily the real wage and the employment level. As regards demand for labour, two major forces need to be considered: replacement and growth of the physical capital stock will provide for a permanent outward shift of the production function. The assumption of a continuous outward shift permits, *ceteris paribus*, to view the labour demand curve as being inversely sloped, as would be the case under increasing returns to scale. The second influence on demand is given by shrinking production in public sector enterprises, offsetting to a certain degree the effect of improved physical capital. Since the decline of output in public enterprises may decrease, while the production function shifts continuously outward, the offset diminishes. Hence, both labour demand and supply could be upward sloping. This may illustrate instability of labour market equilibria during transition and shows that shocks to labour demand can result in larger real wage adjustment required to restore equilibrium than would be the case with a labour demand curve under decreasing returns to scale, underlining the importance of real wage flexibility.[26] Another conclusion suggested by this model is that, in the medium-term, measured unemployment may not decrease by as much as employment rises, because the labour force could increase.

Turning to the efficiency wage theory, whose commonest version states that the difficulty of directly monitoring work effort causes employers to pay real wages above that level which would be compatible with full employment, its contribution to a theoretical solution of the unemployment problem in Eastern Europe appears marginal. However, it points to the need to introduce incentives for employees not to shirk, for instance by means of salaries partly tied to group effort as discussed in the industrial relations literature. Hence, a real wage level incompatible with full employment may be prevented.

The insider-outsider theory would call for ways to provide outsiders (the unemployed) with a voice in wage negotiations. The curtailments of unemployment compensation in Eastern Europe may be assumed to have contributed to a strengthening of this voice. When following the theory one should, however, consider that measures which were conceived of as increasing the power of outsiders could lead to a strengthening of the position of employers relative to the employed without necessarily resulting in dampened wage growth and higher employment. Theoretically, formal representation of outsiders in wage negotiations would be called for.

Finally, the mentioned explanation provided by Solow (1990) for persistence of unemployment, namely society's aversion to a high degree of competition on the labour market, implies that if a lower unemployment rate was achieved, then it would not result in accelerated inflation. Hence, a case for incomes policy could arise, because the issue of its sustainability would be absent. Although Eastern European societies are evidently not less opposed to Hobbesian competition on the labour market than Western societies, there are arguments which call into question the potential support incomes policy could provide to reducing unemployment in Eastern Europe. These are mainly three: first, the experience gained in industrial and developing countries concerning macroeconomic adjustment programs taught that restrictive policies, if implemented consistently, can have a positive immediate impact on growth due to their effects on interest rates, the exchange rate, investment and consumption. Aggregate domestic demand may therefore increase, instead of decline, supported by rising exports. Second, incomes policy could lead to less adjustment regarding fiscal and monetary policy if the authorities believe that the policy was effective in promoting growth and employment. Hence, incomes policy may interfere with this consistency. Third, incomes policy may cause tensions, because trade unions could perceive it as promoting an unequal income distribution. The consequences of subjecting trade unions to certain pressure within the context of an incomes policy appear not to have been favourable in industrial countries, underlined by the fact that incomes policy proved not to be sustainable and at the time of its abandonment there has commonly been a period of accelerated wage and price inflation.

To summarize, the theoretical analysis of unemployment and its persistence regarding industrial countries suggests for Eastern Europe to consider the following primary (interdependent) factors identified as explaining unemployment: the organization of the social security system and the extent (including duration) to which benefits, in particular unemployment compensation, are granted; the system of wage bargaining including representation of unemployed; real wage flexibility; labour-management relations including incentives for monitoring work effort; incentives for search activity; changes in taxation affecting the wedge between real consumption and real product wage (indirect taxes, taxes on wages); subsidies that do not aim at reducing distortions. Factors which should not be regarded as causing unemployment are technological progress, growth of the capital stock, and growth of both the labour force and population.

4. Industrial relations system

The above review pointed to the importance of productivity growth for employment, particularly if real wage flexibility is limited. Moreover, integration of Eastern European economies into world markets through relatively low tariff barriers and largely eliminated subsidization implies that production is exposed to international competition and the increasing pace of technological change. The question thus arises whether restrictive macroeconomic policies to facilitate capital formation could be supplemented by measures apt to contribute to long run productivity growth and competitiveness. In light of the argument that labour-management relations may explain long run growth performance better than wage flexibility (Aoki, 1988), the relevance of this question is further raised.[27] While the issue has since long primarily been examined in the industrial relations literature, the period of relatively low productivity growth in most industrial countries since the first oil price shock in 1973 – it has been particularly low when considering the fundamental technological advances (productivity paradox) – triggered extensive research by economists (see, for instance, Baily, 1981; Gordon, 1988). Specifically, changing the way labour is paid or treated may improve the effectiveness of labour inputs: '... a society starting over again to design a pay system to encourage high productivity would be most unlikely to choose the conventional wage system.' (Blinder, 1990, p. 2). The major proposals are profit sharing, employee stock ownership, and participation in management's decision making.

Using a Keynesian macroeconomic framework with utility maximizing consumers and monopolistically competitive firms, Weitzman (1986) showed that a profit-sharing economy may yield unambiguously superior macroeconomic characteristics both in the short and long run. There is a tendency for the economy to remain on the full employment path, even when hit by an adverse shock, because a fall in labour demand will mainly affect profits, not employment. In the long run, output, employment, and the real wage level would be higher compared to a fixed-wage economy. In theory, the profit sharing economy could offer a solution to unemployment and stagflation.[28] Besides its potential macroeconomic stabilizing properties, profit sharing could promote productivity. The empirical evidence may support this view: although many of the numerous studies (case studies, surveys, econometric studies) on the relationship have flaws and some yield weak results, their meta analysis corroborates the hypothesis for profit sharing and productivity to be positively related (Weitzman and Kruse, 1990).[29] The literature appears to suggest that the magnitude of the influence is dependent upon whether firms introduce additional measures providing for limited participation of employees in firms' decision-making. This finding could be interpreted as a Nash solution and would thus have a theoretical underpinning. It could suggest that where labour laws require employees' participation in decision making, a possible precondition exists for profit sharing to raise productivity. However, there may be two basic caveats. The first concerns capital's long run equilibrium share in national income. Only if this share is not adversely affected is it possible for the macroeconomic outcome to be improved. For instance, if the profit share going to labour exceeds the productivity gain, capital's share is reduced and hence investment would tend to be adversely affected. The second question relates to unemployment. It is conceivable for an insider-outsider problem to be amplified, because instability of workers total earnings in connection with close labour-management relations could lead firms to raise wages above the full employment level to compensate for earnings uncertainty. Government action promoting profit sharing, in particular through tax incentives given to both employers and employees, may appear to offer a solution by reducing the wedge between the productivity gain and what accrues to firms and employees. The empirically measured productivity gain through profit sharing (median estimate of 4.4 per cent regarding the studies surveyed by Weitzman and Kruse, 1990), its relatively high significance (the margin of error is near zero), and the potential for (cash or deferred) profit sharing to be a macroeconomic built-in-stabilizer, may suggest that their promotion through tax incentives could improve employment growth. However, given the importance of fiscal adjustment in Eastern European countries so as to reduce inflation, any measures that risk a short run increase in government expenditures, while the beneficial effect on revenues is uncertain, may not be advisable.

Turning to employee stock-ownership plans (ESOP), the empirical evidence is limited and somewhat contradictory (Conte and Svejnar, 1990; Blasi, 1990). There is some evidence supporting the hypothesis for ESOPs to improve a firm's performance if employee participation in decision making is present. However, the evidence as to which forms of participation are most promising is very weak, and, on a theoretical level, participation other than that stemming from ownership of capital is somewhat difficult to justify. Capital ownership by labour may be seen as the fundamental issue ESOP raises in a market economy. In contrast to cash profit sharing, it provides for labour to own capital with the ensuing voting rights, a possibly triggered learning process, and, *ceteris paribus*, a contribution to a more even income distribution. It thus has the potential to mitigate distributional conflict and promote acceptance, on the part of labour, of the fact that structural change requires resource mobility. However, ESOPs imply increased risk-taking by labour. Therefore, in order to promote both ownership of capital by labour and productivity, a profit sharing plan could appear preferable that provides for payments into funds that hold diversified equity.[30] The scheme could receive preferential tax treatment for firms and employees so as to provide incentives. Given the several unambiguously positive external effects, tax incentives could appear warranted, if, unlike in Eastern Europe, the fiscal balance would not be severely burdened.

Turning to the question of worker participation, one may begin by noting that Eastern European countries have, by now, labour laws that provide for a substantial degree of participation, even at relatively small firms. A precondition for factors of production to be mobile is for their owners to be able to control them. It would thus follow that if a society chooses to deviate from this rule it may have to accept a less efficient resource allocation with implications for the rate of growth. Social science research suggests that participatory workplaces tend to raise worker productivity and satisfaction. However, the relationship is not clear.[31] It is argued that labour-hoarding firms pay a subsidy to firms that lay off workers (Levine and Tyson, 1990). Here it is argued that there does not necessarily have to exist a trade-off between resource mobility (which may be inhibited by participation) and productivity (which could be raised by participation). It appears conceivable that the existing labour laws are adhered to by managements in such a way that both goals may be achieved simultaneously, eased transition of resources out of declining industries and high worker productivity. As already mentioned, in a game theoretic context one may argue for worker participation to facilitate a cooperative solution. Levine and Tyson (1990) identify conditions in product, labour, and capital markets which, in their view, can largely explain how firms are encouraged to adopting a participatory system. Here it is hypothesized that if there are factors that promote voluntary adoption of a participatory system then, under the circumstance that the latter is imposed on firms and not a voluntary choice, establishing or promoting these factors may mitigate potential conflicts and facilitate the required structural adjustment. The authors' framework can be summarized as follows: based on the empirically supported premise that a participatory system may have an efficiency – and, perhaps, social welfare advantage, the question is why it is not more common. The explanation could be market failure, particularly for one reason: participatory systems require long term investment into human capital. Markets may not have the ability to identify these investments and would thus be biased against them.[32] Using the authors' framework, the following assessment may be given: voluntary adoption of a participatory system is hampered by shrinking public sector enterprises and the high levels of unemployment. However, owing to the latter, private sector economic activity may not be subject to wage pressure, particularly not regarding external economic activity, which may benefit from wage differentials to competitor countries and productivity growth due to rising capital labour ratios. In the aggregate, these firms face an outward shifting demand curve. Theoretically, growth of both aggregate demand and employment would be promoted if closure of enterprises was permitted that are not economically viable in the long run (Husain, 1992). Actual developments indicate aggregate demand to be stabilized by generally continuously rising exports.

Measures regarding capital markets may be considered. Reducing asymmetrical information, would promote investments in projects with a relatively long pay-off period and thus could also promote investments into human capital.[33] A multitude of measures are available to promote both a lengthening of time horizons (on the part of investors and managements), and a more even distribution of information through direct means or indirectly by facilitating growth of the information production industry. Given the burdens on fiscal balances by incomes support payments, tax incentives (e.g., graduated capital gains tax) may appear questionable. Tax measures that do not burden the fiscal balance (stock voting rights that increase with length of ownership, treating training costs as investments on corporate balance sheets), or postpone the burden (encouraged long run remuneration of managements) could be considered if they do not pose administrative difficulties. Reference to the already mentioned superior Japanese industrial relations system may be appropriate (Levine and Tyson, 1990; Aoki, 1988): important factors identified as promoting long time horizons and the functioning of capital markets appear to be that intangible investments by firms as, for instance, research and development and training are universally recognized as such. This is facilitated by highly respected associations, set up by firms, that offer training and carry out R/D. Perhaps more relevant to the immediate task of facilitating transition, Japan's capital market is characterized by long term associations between institutional investors and firms. Promotion could also take the form of permitting other institutional investors, in particular insurance companies, to invest in equity. If regulations provide for risk diversification, there is no reason to assume this to endanger long run earnings of insurance companies. On the contrary, long run earnings are likely to increase, because return on equity is, in the long run, higher than on bonds carrying less risk, and growth may be promoted, because the supply of risk capital is, *ceteris paribus*, larger.[34] Another related factor is given by the organization of the social security system. A pay-as-you-go system cannot contribute to capital formation and long term institutional investment. By contrast, a system that pays incomes support out of interest and dividends earned on prior accumulated funds performs this role.

In sum, the participatory approach adopted by Eastern European countries raises the question as to mobility of capital if owners do not have control. Participation may not facilitate the task of structural adjustment. The question is whether restrictive policies (to promote macroeconomic stability and thus capital formation) and wage differentials that reflect skill structures (to promote growth of human capital) would be superior means to achieving productivity growth.

5. Policy considerations

When attempting to evaluate unemployment in Eastern Europe it should be recognized that the primary comparative advantage of Eastern European economies may be given by wage costs.[35] Given this restriction, a basic question appears to be: will there be only a single unemployment rate that is compatible with a stable inflation rate (accelerationist view), perhaps unacceptably high to Eastern European societies and possibly associated with persistence of long term unemployment, or may an institutional order be established such that an unemployment rate compatible with societies values, the economies' present major comparative advantage, and a stable very moderate inflation rate evolves? The preceding discussion suggests the following fundamental elements of an institutional order conducive to alignment of wage growth with productivity growth:

(i) Wage bargaining should be centralized with trade unions and employers' federations well coordinated among themselves.[36]

(ii) The social security system should be organized such that it contains a potential insider-outsider problem. (It may appear less relevant whether a system that offers relatively generous unemployment compensation contributes to unemployment through the channel of labour demand or labour supply.) Based on both theoretical reasoning and the empirical evidence regarding industrial countries (the latter being, however, weak) this may require benefits at a moderate level and incentives to raise search activity. Efficiency of search activity could be expected to be promoted through substitution of private employment exchanges for public ones.[37] In general, it should be recognized that since the elements of a social welfare system are interlinked, a change of one element is likely to require changes of others if it is the intention to affect the level of public expenditures and not merely their composition.

(iii) The role of the government may be seen in adjusting the institutional structure such that an insider-outsider problem does not arise. Involvement of the government in wage bargaining bears the potential of contributing to inconsistent policies.

(iv) The institutional order could also include promotion of profit sharing through tax incentives, since it bears the potential to raise productivity growth and thus the employment level. It may contribute to improved labour management relations. Profit sharing could be organized in form of employee owned funds which, in turn, hold diversified equity so as to promote the supply of risk capital. However, since tax incentives may be required to reduce the risks inherent in profit sharing (lower profit shares and contribution to an insider-outsider problem), and given that adjustment of fiscal balances may have to be viewed as a priority, tax incentives during transition may not be advisable.

(v) As regards lengthening of time horizons, measures affecting the capital market (besides restrictive policies and positive ex-post real interest rates) could

108

prove most effective. Pronounced informational asymmetry during transition until long term relationships between investors and borrowers are established impairs the central role of capital markets in allocating resources. Hence, in addition to improvements of financial system regulation and extensive disclosure requirements for firms, it could prove beneficial to encourage private activity in the information industry (which assesses creditworthiness). Further measures such as stock voting rights that increase with length of ownership, training costs treated as investments on corporate balance sheets, encouraged long run remuneration of managements, permission for insurance companies to invest in equity, may be considered. The goal may be seen in promoting ties between investors and borrowers. In addition, it could be argued that the larger the aggregate size of institutional investors, the larger, *ceteris paribus*, the supply of risk capital. Hence, the proposal of creating a social security capital fund.

Present circumstances suggest the consideration of two further aspects that are not directly related to the institutional order:

Reduction of remaining barriers to allocational efficiency (potential subsidization of public enterprises through commercial banks and tariffs), raises the questions as to the feasibility of further substitution of 'bad' loans in banks' balance sheets and tariff reduction. The former problem is discussed in Section 3.4 below. Subsidies to the housing market to improve labour mobility appear warranted if they do not impair the priority of reducing fiscal deficits. Finally, since increases in taxation that affect the wedge between the product and consumption wage (wage taxation – including social security contributions, indirect taxes) may be incident to some degree and for a considerable period on profits, it would follow that such changes (including their announcement), should be carefully considered.[38]

However, given the primary goal of achieving growth of the capital labour ratio, which may be expected to entail growth of human capital – without government support – if taxation is not based on the egalitarian principle, it could appear preferable to subordinate policies to the aim of containing fiscal deficits. From this perspective, policy measures that may appear optimal in the short run, as, for instance, public works programs which would not be expected to offer particular training effects, may not be seen as optimal in the medium and long run, because their social costs in terms of the impact on growth may outweigh the benefits in terms of an immediate reduction of unemployment. Since scarcity of capital poses a constraint on employment growth in Eastern Europe, improving efficiency of the financial system will raise employment as discussed in the following section.

Notes

1 Excess labour demand was caused by weak budget constraints for enter-prises, i.e. subsidized factor demand, resulting in insatiable demand for investment purposes, labour hoarding tendencies and thus disguised unem-ployment.

2 The relatively lower initial rise of unemployment in Romania may be largely attributable to extensive use of short-time working arrangements, early retirement schemes and measures to postpone lay-offs in public enter-prises.

3 In Bulgaria, only about 50 per cent of persons who are registered as unem-ployed collect unemployment compensation (in contrast to about 80 per cent in the other countries). One reason for this appears to be that these persons find employment in the private sector and do not collect benefits because this would trigger a loss or reduction of other social benefits. It underlines, however, both the difficulty in interpreting measured unem-ployment in Eastern Europe and to provide a meaningful definition of unemployment.

4 The main characteristics of unemployment in Eastern Europe can be sum-marized as follows, subject to caveats mentioned below: unemployment resulted nearly entirely from the output decline since early 1990 which, in turn, affected industrial sectors relatively most in all countries, and the sec-tors agriculture, construction and services in varying degrees. As a by-product of the rise in unemployment, regional differentials increased. Unemployment is concentrated on less skilled workers of prime age and workers with vocational training; it has a larger impact on school-leavers and other new entrants than on older people; women are generally more affected than men; the average length of unemployment spells appears to have risen; the highest unemployment levels are generally in regions with heavy industries or mining. The caveats result from statistical weaknesses. Two major data sources are available: administrative data and survey results. Regarding some characteristics, the data of these sources differ sig-nificantly. However, there are also remarkable consistencies between them, as found, for instance, with respect to Hungary (OECD, 1992, p. 251).

5 Since elements of social expenditures are closely inter-linked, the reduction of one of them can cause an increase in another. This is one aspect of the complexity of an analysis. Perraudin's (1993) contribution regarding pen-sion and unemployment benefit reform in Poland underlines the necessity to consider cuts in pensions and unemployment benefits carefully so as to limit the impact on welfare – including adverse effects on poverty. The analysis is briefly elaborated on in Section 4.3 below.

6 Population growth is very moderate in all Eastern European countries and appears to have declined somewhat during transition.

7   The Table does not distinguish between the Czech and Slovak Republics. As explained in the following, it provides, however, significant information as to explaining the divergence of the levels of unemployment in these two Republics from the average level in Eastern Europe. Note that statistical weaknesses account for a substantial margin of error regarding these indices. Information on real product wages would be important but reliable estimates for Bulgaria and Romania are not available.

8   Major reasons for this have been the large adverse terms of trade shock during 1990 and 1991 and cuts in consumer good subsidies.

9   Details are provided in Aghevli et. al., 1992.

10 In industrial countries employment tends to follow closely the investment ratio (investment as per cent of GNP). For instance, in Germany, during the past two decades this has been the case with a lag, in general, of less than a quarter.

11 The feasible level may be defined as the one that corresponds to the marginal product of labour in the aggregate. One way of calculating it for a given economy would be to multiply aggregate capital employed with a long term interest rate and deducting this amount from national income. It is an ethical question whether one accepts the marginal productivity doctrine as 'fair.' Some economists asserted that the 'law' of marginal productivity is fair (see, in particular, Bates (1899)).

12 At the end of 1992, the Czech and Slovak Republics and Hungary abandoned these types of incomes policy mainly owing to their distortionary effects.

13 The question as to the relative importance of physical and human capital during transition may be discussed in the following way: the influence of human capital on the rate of output growth is, for instance, demonstrated in Calvo and Frenkel, 1992. Accumulation of human capital may be seen as a positive function of mainly three variables: wage differentials that reflect differences in skills, the capital/labour ratio due to learning by doing effects and, as discussed in the following Section 4, labour-management relations which affect work effort. Hence, growth of human capital could be promoted through capital formation and a progressive personal income tax scale whose slope is rather moderate. Public programs providing for retraining could be, to some degree, substituted for by permitting wage differentials to emerge. A case for government action may then be present only with regard to improvement of labour-management relations, as discussed in Section 4. Commonly, the contribution of investment to increases in labour productivity (output per hour of work) is seen as primarily dependent on the respective shares of capital and labour in the economy's total costs. Since labour's share in industrial countries amounts to around 60-70 per cent, measures to make labour inputs more productive are therefore regarded as superior to growth of the capital stock (Blinder,

1990 p. 2)). The caveat of this assessment may be given by rather strong correlation between growth of capital and that of productivity in cross-section analyses regarding industrial countries, which could point to a direct channel between the capital labour ratio and quality of labour inputs. Data regarding capital's share in total costs in Eastern European economies are not available (and even if available they would be unreliable due to growth of the informal sector). It could appear legitimate to assume, however, that wage costs relative to those of capital decreased substantially since 1993 in all countries owing to strengthened incentives for managements of public enterprises to service capital. Assuming relatively high investment ratios in private sectors, a rapid rise of private sectors' share in GDP, and a restructuring of public expenditures such that investments in infrastructure gain importance, Eastern European economies are likely to have a larger share of total costs accounted for by capital inputs compared to industrial countries' average. In addition, growth of capital may also be viewed as the most efficient way to counteract the assessed degradation of the environment during the past decades.

14 Export growth has been relatively strong (geographical redirection of exports and product quality improvements occurred in all countries), private household savings ratios have risen, the adjustment and hence overall performance of public enterprises is widely evaluated as better than expected, and, in general, foreign direct investment accelerated.

15 Specifically, in an intertemporal substitution model the representative economic agent chooses that time path of consumption and leisure which satisfies the following first-order conditions: first, the real wage and the marginal rate of substitution between present leisure and consumption are equated, second, the marginal utility loss from giving up present consumption must equal the marginal utility gain from future consumption, and third, the marginal utility loss of giving up present leisure must equal the marginal utility gain of future leisure.

16 Layard, Nickel and Jackman (1991, p. 512) review briefly the empirical literature. See also Summers (1990, pp. 160-186).

17 As of early 1993, in Romania a bankruptcy law has not been enacted.

18 Those sectors in decline that still receive subsidies could shrink without forcing workers to change activities, owing to natural attrition.

19 As has been documented, the protection of agriculture causes significant income losses in industrial countries, particularly in the European Communities (EC) and Japan. For instance, in Germany the costs of protection provided for the agricultural sector (including subsidies) exceed value added generated in this sector. The root of protection may be seen in the aim of countries to maintain a certain degree of self-sufficiency. The concept of self-sufficiency, however, contradicts the principle of division of labour. Integration of the former CMEA countries into world markets

since 1990, which extends to the political sphere, could be regarded as providing an opportunity to review policies directed at maintaining self-sufficiency. Although it would be difficult to assess accurately the extent to which agricultural production in Western and Eastern European countries was affected by a hypothetical phasing out of these subsidies and reduction of tariffs and quotas concerning agricultural goods, in the long run the impact on national incomes would be positive. The Partnership Treaties concluded between the EC on the one hand, and the Czech and Slovak Republics, Hungary, and Poland, on the other, exclude agricultural goods from the eventual establishment (within ten years since 1992) of free movement of labour, services, and capital – including liberalized settlement rights for businesses.

20 To ascertain a ceiling of this burden, it could appear reasonable to add employment in public enterprises with substantial and continuing arrears and multiply it by the per capita cost of compensation and retraining.

21 However, real wage flexibility is not sufficient to avoid unemployment: although those countries with relatively low unemployment tend to have relatively flexible real wage levels, there are exceptions.

22 The degree of estimated real wage flexibility in Japan is highest among industrial countries (Layard, Nickel, Jackman, 1991, Table 2, p. 407). However, with respect to the discussion in the following Section 4 it may be noted that this flexibility does not appear to be mainly a result of Japan's bonus system (profit-sharing) which is applied in large companies. These companies employ only about 40 per cent of the labour force and a significant part of the bonuses appears to be fixed. Wage flexibility may be accounted for mainly by the small-firm sector.

23 A real wage level which is too high can be a cause for unemployment just as wage pressure with an unchanged real wage level: in the latter case, the total number of hours worked remains unchanged but is distributed among fewer employees so that yearly real pay per worker increases. Sachs'(1983) conclusion, that the decreasing aggregate profit shares in many Western European GDP's – following the oil price shocks in the 1970s – have been a primary cause for unemployment, triggered a still ongoing discussion regarding the question as to whether real wage levels are too high. However, in either case, the importance lies with wage pressure, defined as a real wage target on the part of trade unions above its feasible level.

24 The fact that real wage flexibility tends to promote employment does not imply that falling nominal wages during a recession promote growth. In general, it is the absence of Walrasian market clearing which may largely explain reduced business-cycle variability since the Second World War (DeLong and Summers, 1984). In particular, since Keynes, consideration of the deflationary effect of falling nominal wages and thus of a higher real interest rate – which may outweigh any expansionary Pigou effect – , sug-

gests to use the price level, or, as explained below, profit sharing in engineering real wage adjustment. Profit sharing could be preferable, because the use of the price level bears risks which may not be ascertainable. On a modern view of wage flexibility, that confirms the importance of real wage flexibility but questions, in accordance with Keynes, nominal downward flexibility, see Hahn and Solow, 1986.

25 The discussion concentrates on less skilled labour and the labour market is therefore seen as rather homogeneous.

26 The potential employment level effect on labour supply tends, however, to dampen instability.

27 The importance of real wage flexibility and thus wage pressure for growth and employment in Eastern Europe should, however, be seen as dominant, because the primary comparative advantage of Eastern European economies may be given by wage levels. Improved labour management relations and industrial relations systems should therefore be seen as means to promote real wage flexibility and productivity so as to raise the employment level through a rise of the feasible real wage.

28 Japan's economy is often cited as being characterized by profit sharing. This view is incorrect (see Note 25). Weitzman's model does not appear to explain Japan's low unemployment, because output is not stable, prices are not only affected by demand, excess demand for labour is relatively low and base wages do not appear to be the primary determinant of employment. For a discussion see: Layard, Nickel, and Jackman, 1991, p. 72.

29 Most of the empirical analysis of profit sharing plans in the United States and Europe concerns deferred profit sharing trusts which hold employer securities. In these countries cash profit sharing is rare. Hence, in practice, the border between profit sharing and employee stock ownership is blurred.

30 Further beneficial macroeconomic effects of this aspect of an industrial relations system appear certain: higher demand for equity, implying improved incentives for firms to choose a legal form which is accepted by the equity funds, as, for instance, the stock-holding company. Such firms, in turn, commonly provide information of better quality regarding their financial standing and growth (owing to legal requirements) than companies of other legal form. Hence, market transparency and mobility of capital is promoted. Moreover, promotion of private savings in the form of equity affects positively capital formation and firms financial soundness.

31 Levine and Tyson (1990) conclude that the participatory systems most effective in raising productivity are profit sharing, long-term employment relations, measures that provide for group cohesiveness, and guaranteed individual rights.

32 Specifically, the authors' framework has three pillars: first, with imperfect information, capital markets cannot be expected to provide funds for investments in hard-to-monitor projects. To the extent that funds are avail-

able for a participatory firm, the latter faces, however, relatively high capital costs: equity costs are, *ceteris paribus*, higher than for conventional firms, since the owners have, by definition, less than complete control over capital and decision making. In addition, given pronounced asymmetric information with regard to investments into human capital, the debt to equity ratio a participatory firm can support without facing an increase in borrowing costs may be lower than for a conventional firm. Lowering of capital costs requires a more symmetric distribution of information and thus long term relationships between firms and providers of capital. A second characteristic conducive to participation is seen in stability of the demand curve a firm faces. If it is rather unstable, exhibits relatively large, frequent shifts, the participatory firm, which aims at avoiding lay offs, faces relatively high costs. Hence, participatory firms have a better chance to evolve in economies where active demand management policy is pursued (e.g. Sweden). Third, it is argued that a relatively low average unemployment level, narrow wage dispersion, and universal just cause dismissal policy favour participatory firms.

33 Informational asymmetries may be pronounced because investor/firm relationships have yet to stabilize on the basis of the new relative prices since 1990. In addition, to the extent that uncertainty about the future course of 'fundamentals' and changes in taxation is pervasive, time horizons could tend to be relatively short. Short time horizons and the resulting efficiency losses can be subsumed under the aspect of market transparency whose improvement constitutes a case for government action in any market economy. Informational asymmetries raise moral hazard and adverse selection issues as reviewed in Section 3 below.

34 The indirect coercion of insurance companies (through prudential regulations) to hold mainly government bonds can be considered a tax levied on capital market borrowers resulting in a distortion: government expenditures are subsidized with capital market borrowers paying this implicit tax.

35 To ascertain how Eastern Europe will be integrated into world trade, it is necessary to make assumptions as to the relative importance of factors which drive trade, such as factor endowment differences, industry-wide technological differences, product differentiation (imperfect competition), and economies of scale. Given the above cited EC association agreements, tariffs concerning trade between Hungary, the Czech and Slovak Republics and Poland, on the one hand, and Western Europe, on the other, will be abolished by 2002. (Customs duties and quantitative restrictions on exports will be abolished by 1997). Relatively low-wages in Eastern Europe may, for some time, remain the primary determinant of export growth. Regarding Bulgaria and Romania, tariffs could have an additional significant influence. Presently, in all countries, except Bulgaria (who has a somewhat lower share), about 55-65 per cent of exports are directed to the

EC, the trend still being increasing. From this a policy goal may follow, namely to maintain the comparative advantage of relatively low unit labour costs, while simultaneously improving product differentiation in the wake of a rise in the capital labour ratio. For an example of an initially labour surplus economy (Singapore), that experienced a low-wage, export-led growth path whose structure changed to one of high-wage, technology- and skill-intensive, higher value-added activities, see Chadha, 1991.

36 Joint economic analysis prior to wage bargaining (as successfully applied in Scandinavian countries) may be promoted. Labour laws could be amended to provide for both 'peace agreements,' hindering strikes, as successfully applied in Switzerland and Germany, and mediation if bargaining does not yield results within a given period.

37 The empirical evidence suggests that public employment agencies in industrial countries may not be relatively efficient intermediaries (see, for instance, Layard et. al., 1991, p. 240).

38 The above made suggestion to switch from a pay-as-you-go social security system to a capital fund based system, which would require extra financing, would thus require to consider a trade off between its long run beneficial effect and potential short run costs through a possibly increased real product wage, if financed through higher social security contributions.

3 Financial system evolution

1. The problem

In a stylized centrally-planned economy, besides assuming the role of issuing currency, the central bank acts as the main credit and deposit bank. It controls the allocation of credit and foreign exchange in fulfilment of the central plan. Aggregate savings and investment in the economy are largely determined by this central plan and not the result of decisions on the part of private households and firms.[1] Hence, the financial system assumes a passive role and cannot significantly contribute to growth. Interest rates are arbitrarily fixed and do not have an allocative function. Fiscal deficits are financed through the central bank whose liabilities side shows a corresponding increase in either of three items: private savings (deposits), money creation (raising excess demand with prices fixed) and/or external borrowing. Existing banks assist the central bank in foreign trade financing, collecting deposits, allocating credit, and carrying out the insurance business.[2] There are no legal spot markets for bonds, equity, foreign exchange, financial derivatives, and no futures markets to hedge risk.[3] Indirect monetary policy instruments are absent. Thus, besides the question regarding implementation of the legal order required to enable financial intermediation to evolve, creation of a financial system in a formerly centrally-planned economy with open borders for trade (current account convertibility plus liberalized foreign direct investment and repatriation of profits) means, foremost, that financial institutions, be they private or public, have to manage the basic risks associated with financial activity.[4] Whether the evolution of financial intermediation under liberalized interest rates can meet, first, its economic function (channelling of resources into activities associated with the highest social return with risk-taking entrepreneurship being promoted through optimal distribution of risk among domestic and foreign market participants), and, second, the goal of full exploitation of economies of scale and scope with stability of the system being maintained, may be seen primarily as a function of the degree to which these basic risks are managed – which, in turn, is largely dependent on financial market regulation. As discussed in Section 4 below, both the degree of macroeconomic stability and regulation of financial markets largely determine the latter's contribution to growth and thus employment. The fact that Eastern European financial systems are bank-based has, in turn, implications for both the allocation of capital and efficacy of monetary policy.

2. Evolution of financial systems since 1990

Eastern European countries opted for universal banking systems. Although there is dissension as to the relative advantages of this type of system (employed in most Western European countries) compared to the legal separation between the securities and commercial banking business (e.g., Japan, United States), theoretical reasoning and the experience, particularly during the 1980s, could suggest that universal banking offers advantages with respect to both the financial systems' stability and costs of intermediation (Appendix I).

Tables 3.1 and 3.2 provide an overview regarding the evolution of financial systems in Eastern Europe and their regulation. The capital markets are bank-based with securities markets very limited in breadth and depth. The banking systems evolved in the following way: prior to transition, collecting of deposits, on the one hand, and extension of credit, on the other, was carried out by different 'branches' of the central bank. Hence, there were, in principal, two ways to commercialize them: leaving this structural form in place and to grant independence to the branches, possibly splitting them up, or to distribute the assets and liabilities among newly created institutions. All considered countries, except the former Czech and Slovak Federal Republic, opted for the second approach. In Bulgaria and Hungary, the reform of the banking system was implemented already prior to the adoption of structural adjustment and reform programs. All countries, again with the exception of the former Czech and Slovak Federal Republic, established several successor (universal) banks and specialized financial institutions (government owned). Very few of these have a network of branches enabling them to operate nation-wide. In Bulgaria, Hungary and Romania the new banks were set up along industry lines. In Poland they are regional banks. In the Czech and Slovak Republics, the first mentioned method of commercialization was chosen, with loans to large public enterprises mainly transferred to the 'Investment Bank.' Hence, in each of the two Republics there are now three dominating banks: one commercial bank, one savings bank, and one investment bank, where the problem of non-performing loans is concentrated in the latter, which is a unique case in Eastern Europe. In all countries, the commercialized successor institutions of the former central banks are naturally dominating as regards market share. They are still government-owned, or the government holds

118

Table 3.1

Selected Eastern European countries: characteristics of financial systems in 1993

	Capital Market	Money Market	Payments System	Stock Exchange	Futures Markets	Credit Rating Agencies
Bulgaria	Bank-based; savings and loan bank; joint-stock commercial banks, the largest ones being government owned; specialized financial institutions; foreign banks admitted.	*Inter-bank*: call-money. *Official*: treasury bills; short-term treasury bonds; bills of exchange; repurchase agreements.	Clearing through State Bank (computerized, real time).	Planned.	None.	None.
Czech Republic	Bank-based; joint-stock commercial banks (the government being a minority shareholder in the largest one); one savings and loan bank (government being a majority shareholder); one specialized institution (government holding a minority share); a number of mutual funds (owned by banks) foreign banks admitted.	*Inter-bank*: call-money. *Official*: treasury bills; short-term treasury bonds; bills of exchange; repurchase agreements.	Clearing through State Bank (computerized, real time).	Established in 1993.	None	None.
Hungary	Bank-based; joint-stock commercial banks, with the government holding mainly minority shares in the largest banks; savings-cooperatives specialized by region; specialized financial institutions; foreign banks admitted; offshore banks.	*Inter-bank*: call-money. *Official*: treasury bills; short-term treasury bonds; bills of exchange; repurchase agreements.	Clearing through State Bank (computerized, real time).	Established in 1990.	None.	None.
Poland	Bank-based; joint-stock commercial banks (the largest are 9 successor institutions of previous 'mono-bank' system which operate regionally and are government owned but intended to be privatized); state cooperative banks; specialized institutions; foreign banks admitted.	*Inter-bank*: call-money. *Official*: treasury bills; treasury bonds (1 and 3 years maturity); bills of exchange; repurchase agreements.	Clearing through State Bank.	Established in 1991.	None.	None.
Slovak Republic	Bank-based; joint-stock commercial banks (government being a minority shareholder in the largest); one savings and loan bank (government being a majority shareholder); one specialized institution (government holding a minority share); foreign banks admitted.	*Inter-bank*: call-money. *Official*: treasury bills; bills of exchange; repurchase agreements.	Clearing through State Bank.	Established in 1993.	None.	None.
Romania	Bank-based; joint-stock commercial banks the largest of which being government owned; savings and loan bank (government owned); credit cooperatives; specialized financial institutions; foreign banks admitted.	*Inter-bank*: call-money. *Official*: bills of exchange.	Clearing through State Bank. Licensing of inter-bank clearing houses planned.	Planned.	None.	None.

Sources: IMF staff, various national publications.

a majority share.[5] However, all governments decided in favour of financial intermediation eventually to be undertaken privately, implying for the public to become, in principle, a minority shareholder in these successor institutions, with some exceptions regarding specialized banks (e.g., Savings Banks in the Czech and Slovak Republics). Establishment of private banks was permitted relatively quickly following the adoption of reform programs. Initially, the paid-in capital requirements were generally and deliberately set relatively low so as to facilitate establishments which, however, in connection with inadequate banking supervision, resulted in some dubious banks to fail. In all considered countries a large number of small private banks exists (operating locally). The payments systems, whose importance lies in their potential to facilitate contagion of materializing risk, are being adjusted to international standards mainly through central banks. Foreign banks are admitted, but very few are operating. Stock exchanges were established except in Bulgaria and Romania. Securities markets exist for government bonds and bills (except in Romania), with short term papers dominating. Privately issued securities exist in the form of certificates of deposit (issued by banks), which are, in principle, tradable, and very limited amounts of equity in the Czech and Slovak Republics, Hungary and Poland. Borrowing by firms remains, however, nearly entirely restricted to bank and inter enterprise credit.

Table 3.2 provides an overview regarding advances in financial system regulation. The countries decided differently on the crucial question of the degree of independence granted to the central bank. The law on the Czech National Bank appears to provide for relative autonomy of the institution with respect to both domestic price stability and the external value of the currency. The law is unique among the considered Eastern European countries. Although rather similar, the Law on the National Bank of Slovakia contains ambiguities, in particular concerning the dismissal of members of the governing board of the bank. The Law on the National Bank of Poland stipulates that extension of credit by the National Bank to the Government has to be coordinated among these two parties: since the introduction of the law in 1989, these negotiated limits do not appear to have been binding. The Laws on the Bulgarian National Bank and the National Bank of Romania do not appear to confer relative independence to them as regards control of the money supply.

Supervision of financial intermediaries has been implemented in all considered countries. As already emphasized, the question is, however, to what extent a moral hazard problem still exists. As demonstrated in Appendix II. it is fundamental: until experiences with financial liberalization during the 1980s in several developing countries were gained, it was mainstream theoretical reasoning (in response mainly to McKinnon's (1973) contribution) that eliminating 'financial repression,' (defined as distorted domestic money and capital markets through interest rate regulation, credit ceilings, high reserve requirements etc.), and permitting real interest rates to become positive, would result in higher savings and investment. However, this reasoning did not account for moral hazard

Table 3.2
Selected Eastern European countries: characteristics of financial system regulation in 1993

	Central Bank Independence	Banking Supervision [a]	Deposit Insurance	Regulation of Interest Rates	Elimination of "bad" Debt in Banks' Balance Sheets	Regulation of Securities Market
Bulgaria	Law on Bulgarian National Bank (BNB) provides for limited degree of independence of the BNB.	Regulation of items a,b,c, since 1990; improved regulation of a,b,c, and new regulation of d, e, f to be introduced in 1993	Planned.	Liberalized in 1991.	Plan to recapitalize banks through write-off against BNP deposits, where BNP would be compensated by government securities; non-performing pre-1990 loans planned to be government guaranteed; banks would be prohibited to continue lending to state enterprises in arrears.	Planned.
Czech Republic	Law on Czech National Bank (CNB) provides for a high degree of independence of the CNB.[b]	Items a,b,c,d,e,f regulated since 1992 with the aim to abide by BIS standards.	Planned.	Liberalized in 1991; moral suasion policy regarding deposit rates to counteract lack of competition and reduce borrowing-lending spreads.	Creation of Consolidation Bank in 1991 (state-owned; non-profit) to acquire a share of bad debt; recapitalization of commercial banks; reliance on capital adequacy requirements and doubtful loans provisioning requirements.	Laws of limited scope enacted.
Hungary	Law on National Bank of Hungary (NBH) provides for relative independence of the NBH. The Central Bank is not autonomous with regard to exchange rate policy.	Items a,b,c,d,e,f regulated since 1992 in accordance with BIS standards.	Introduced in 1993.	Liberalized gradually during 1987-1991.	Reliance on capital adequacy requirements and provisioning requirements for doubtful loans.	Laws of limited scope enacted.
Poland	National Bank of Poland (NBP) not legally independent, but limits imposed on lending by the NBP to the Government.	Items a,b,c,d,e,f regulated since 1992 with the aim to abide by BIS standards.	Planned.	Liberalized in 1990; moral suasion policy to counteract uncompetitive market behavior and reduce lending-deposit spreads.	Consideration of recapitalization of banks. Reliance on capital adequacy requirements and doubtful loans provisioning requirements.	Laws of limited scope enacted.
Slovak Republic	Law on National Bank of the Slovakia (NBS) provides for limited degree of independence of the NBS.[c]	Items a,b,c,d,e,f regulated since 1992 with the aim to abide by BIS standards.	Planned.	Liberalized in 1991; moral suasion policy to counteract uncompetitive market behavior and reduce lending-deposit spreads.	Creation of Consolidation Bank in 1991 to acquire share of bad debt. Recapitalization of commercial banks. Reliance on capital adequacy requirements and provisioning requirements for doubtful loans.	Laws of limited scope enacted.
Romania	Law on National Bank of Romania (NBR) provides for limited degree of independence of the NBR.	Regulation of items a,b,c,d,e,f to be introduced in 1993.	Planned.	Liberalized in 1991; temporary limits imposed on spreads between lending and deposit rates.	'Global Compensation' scheme (completed Jan 1992) provided for government guaranteed loans from banks to enterprises in the amount of their arrears; since then arrears accumulated again; plan for system to monitor financial situation enterprises on a monthly basis, early application of bankruptcy procedures (following approval of bankruptcy law by parliament planned for 1993), requirement for state-owned enterprises to charge market interest on inter-enterprise credits (to be monitored).	Planned.

a Capital adequacy = a
Liquidity = b
Concentration of loan portfolio = c
Currency risk = d
Loan loss provisions = e
Off-balance sheet transactions = f
Term-structure risk = g

b Law sets limit for short term credit to the Government. Responsibility for exchange rate policy explicitly granted to the Central Bank. Members of governing body of the Central Bank may be recalled only on account of well defined reasons.

c Law sets limit for short term credit to the Government. Responsibility for exchange rate policy explicitly granted to the Central Bank. Reasons for recalling of members of governing body of the Central Bank not defined.

Sources: IMF staff; various national publications, unpublished national documents.

as later recognized by McKinnon (1988) and others. The problem of moral hazard may be seen to be amplified owing to theoretical advances in asset pricing, options, futures markets, and financial derivatives, which resulted in an unbundling of risks and their trading so that risk taking was facilitated and risk containment on the part of financial intermediaries rendered more difficult. Regarding Eastern European countries, this question should be seen independently of the twin problem of 'bad' loans in banks' balance sheets and generally still rising inter-enterprise arrears: markets for risk are likely to evolve rapidly and thus would in any case confront the authorities with the question as to how moral hazard may be prevented from materializing, or put differently, how excessive risk taking may be prevented on the part of financial intermediaries or other economic agents that would not appear to be the most able to bear risk. Table 3.2 shows that banks' capital adequacy, liquidity, concentration of loan portfolios, currency risk, provisioning for loan losses, and off-balance sheet business are, in principle, regulated. However, the degree of regulation varies significantly and only Hungary and the Czech and Slovak Republics require banks to meet the BIS rules (which appear not sufficient as discussed in Section 4) within a stipulated period.

Introduction of deposit insurance has been introduced in Hungary in early 1993 and is planned in all other considered countries. The economic implication of deposit insurance is that it contributes to preventing bank runs and thus also panics and liquidity crises as assessed in Section 4.

Regulation of interest rates has, in principle, been abandoned. The persistence of relatively large spreads between lending and deposit rates (Table 3.3) caused the authorities in all countries to pursue some form of moral suasion aiming at reducing these spreads. Interpretation of interest rate spreads prevailing in a given financial system is difficult in general, because the number of factors involved is large. In the theoretical case of an economy where markets are competitive and complete and where market participants have perfect foresight, risk would not exist so that spreads would reflect merely the liquidity premium and transaction costs. Introducing the following factors can explain a rise in spreads: barriers to entry (or uncompetitive markets for other reasons such as additional regulations), risk, taxation, moral suasion policies. Risk taking, in turn, may be promoted through materializing moral hazard. Which of these factors dominates is difficult to assess. Appendix II concludes that although Eastern European countries are in danger of experiencing excessive risk taking on the part of financial intermediaries, this has not (yet) resulted in increased bank lending, because enterprises could borrow less expensive from other firms. If this channel would not exist, it could appear that a risk is present such that the experiences of several developing countries which liberalized interest rates in the early 1980s and subsequently were faced with bank failures, could be repeated. Theoretically, this may be the case, particularly where economic agents expect inflation to remain relatively high.[6] It should also be noted

Table 3.3

Selected Eastern European countries: margin between lending and deposit interest rates 1991-92

(As percentage points)

	1991									1992									
	Apr	May	Jun	Jul	Aug	Sep	Oct	Nov	Dec	Jan	Feb	Mar	Apr	May	Jun	Jul	Aug	Sep	Oct
Bulgaria																			
Working capital [a]	19.8	19.8	20.6	17.3	19.0	18.3	18.4	19.0	19.6	20.5	20.9	21.1	21.0	20.9	21.4	20.3	19.7	18.8	18.4
Czech and Slovak Federal Republic																			
Working capital [b]	7.9	8.3	6.1	6.4	6.2	6.3	6.6	6.8	7.4	6.0	5.1	5.1	7.5	7.0	7.2	7.4	7.5	7.3	—
Building and consumer loans [c]	-4.1	-4.7	-5.0	-2.3	-4.1	-4.0	-3.7	-3.4	-3.7	-3.2	-3.8	-3.8	-2.0	-1.8	-1.9	-1.3	-0.7	-0.3	—
Poland																			
Working capital [d]	26.0	14.5	14.5	20.0	17.5	17.7	15.7	15.7	15.7	15.7	13.0	13.0	10.2	10.2	10.2	10.2	10.2	10.2	10.2
Hungary																			
Working capital [e]	6.3	4.2	4.6	4.8	4.7	4.7	3.8	3.8	4.4	4.1	4.7	5.7	6.8	6.8	7.7	9.7	11.4	10.7	11.2

Source: International Monetary Fund, Data Fund.

a   Margin of average actual cost of funds borrowed for working capital over average deposit rate.
b   Margin of average actual cost of funds borrowed for working capital over average rate on savings accounts.
c   Margin of average actual cost of building and consumer loans over average rate on savings accounts.
d   Margin of average actual cost of funds borrowed for working capital over average deposit rate.
e   Margin of average actual cost of funds borrowed for working capital over average rate on deposits with less than one year maturity.

that only the successor banks of the former central banks are burdened with a relatively high share of nonperforming loans. With respect to these banks, relatively high spreads could reflect primarily risks borne. However, it could appear reasonable, to assume the spreads also to be caused by banks exploiting any given monopolistic position.

The spreads may pose a problem with respect to national savings and investment: dependent on the elasticity of private savings with respect to the interest rate, the higher the spread, *ceteris paribus*, the lower tend savings to be. On the other hand, relatively high spreads may promote loan loss provisions enabling banks to attain positive or rising net worth, thus stabilizing the economy. Since governments remain the dominant owners of those banks that hold the 'bad' debt, distribution of their earnings can be influenced, as mentioned, such that this debt is written off. Both borrowers who service debt and depositors would thus bear the burden of paying off non-performing loans.[7] In this context, the evolution of banks' loanable funds may be noted. If deposit rates were 'depressed' (particularly if they yield an ex-ante negative return) one would expect, *ceteris paribus*, an adverse effect on the supply of deposits. Table 3.4 provides weak evidence confirming this hypothesis. The ratio of M2 to GDP does not only indicate velocity, but it is also an indicator of the base available to banks in extending loans. Here M2 includes foreign currency deposits which rose in all countries. This may reflect the good export performance. The Table shows that three countries experienced a rise of this ratio in 1992 (the former Czech and Slovak Federal Republic, Hungary, and Poland), whereas in Bulgaria and Romania the decline during the previous year continued, despite rising for-

Table 3.4
Selected Eastern European countries:
indicator of bank loanable funds 1989-92

(Ratio of M2 to GDP)[a]

		1989	1990	1991	1992 [b]
Bulgaria		1.01	1.04	0.72	0.61
Czech and Slovak Federal Republic		0.73	0.68	0.64	0.74
Poland		0.89	0.32	0.29	0.36
Hungary [c]		0.41	0.48	0.59	0.66
Romania		0.50	0.55	0.37	0.22
Memorandum:	1991				
United States	0.60				
Japan	1.11				

Source: International Monetary Fund, Data Fund.

a M2 defined as average annual money plus quasi-money stock.
b Estimates.
c Includes bonds and savings notes.

eign currency holdings. To use real deposit interest rates in explaining this development does not appear to suffice, because, on a yearly average ex-post basis, these appear to have been generally negative. Unobservable inflationary expectations may be seen as an important factor explaining these developments,[8] since they are likely to result in economizing on money holdings. This effect is reinforced if deposit rates are depressed due to a persistence of relatively large interest rate spreads. With a declining M2/GDP ratio, and given underdeveloped securities markets, credit supply as a share of GDP will, *ceteris paribus*, decline with an adverse impact on growth. However, since banks did not, in general, utilize fully the imposed credit ceilings, this decrease in loanable funds in Bulgaria and Romania cannot explain relatively tight lending on the part of banks. The explanation for this could be seen in a decrease of demand for bank credit associated with rising inter-enterprise arrears (Appendix II).

Regulation of securities markets in Eastern Europe is emerging. Its economic meaning is to limit monopolistic practices and promote a more even information distribution which implies an improved resource allocation. The regulations concern the primary and secondary markets for corporate equity and bonds. The goal should be for the public to perceive these markets (as any market) as 'fair' in order to promote confidence in them and thus savings and investment. While it may be argued that without secondary markets the evolution of primary markets could be inhibited, it should be acknowledged that, independent of the situation in Eastern Europe, the importance lies with promoting the former, in particular the market for equity, because capital is raised and allocated only on primary markets. It is their functioning that influences resource allocation and less so the functioning of secondary markets.[9]

Finally, the evolution of control of privatized joint stock enterprises becomes an issue of importance. Four cases need to be distinguished. First, private individual owners hold the shares and possibly delegate voting rights to banks where the shares are deposited. Second, the shares are held by mutual funds (which are, in general, owned by banks). Third, banks become owners of enterprises through debt equity swaps, which would raise the question as to whether limits will be imposed on such holdings. Fourth, cross holdings among enterprises dominate. It appears that in the Czech and Slovak Republics emphasis is placed on the first and second case, whereas Poland and Hungary pursue mainly a combination of the first and third method. In Bulgaria and Romania, the process may still have to be decided on. Before evaluating these developments, the following section reviews performance criteria of a financial system.

3. Efficiency of a financial system

Economic theory has established many concepts of efficiency. With respect to a financial system, Tobin (1984) distinguishes four concepts: information-arbi-

trage efficiency, fundamental-valuation efficiency, full-insurance efficiency, and functional efficiency. On the basis of these criteria, the following characteristics may define 'efficient' fulfilment of the economic function of a financial system:
(i) prices of financial instruments behave as a random walk (i.e. there is no systematic trading gain to be expected from using the history of a financial instrument's price),
(ii) prices of financial instruments reflect fundamentals,
(iii) availability of financial instruments enabling economic agents to transfer purchasing power over time and to satisfy their desire to hedge risks,
(iv) a distribution of risks reflecting the ability and willingness of bearers,
(v) selection and monitoring of managers whose investment projects receive financing because they are associated with the highest expected returns,
(vi) provision of payments mechanisms that facilitate transactions, and
(vii) use of production technology that permits intermediation and transactions to be carried out at least costs.

Each of these criteria is subject to extensive research, but it may not be necessary to present details, because the state of financial systems in Eastern Europe does not appear to permit their application. Therefore, the following evaluation focuses on government policies that could be expected to enhance the capability of financial systems to raise and allocate capital, and assesses the likely allocation of resources in a bank-based financial system. Developments on markets for securities and foreign exchange are not discussed.[10] It may be mentioned, however, that adjustment of the regulations concerning securities markets in Eastern Europe to Western standards, in particular with respect to primary securities markets, would be important so as to promote their efficient development.[11]

4. Evaluation of financial system evolution

Before evaluating the developments of financial systems in Eastern Europe, it should be noted that the contribution of a financial system to employment growth lies in the promotion of efficient resource allocation, particularly if the constraint to employment growth is scarcity of capital. With a given volume of savings, improved efficiency of the financial system implies, *ceteris paribus*, increased capital formation.

The evaluation of financial systems' evolution may begin by elaborating on the degree of independence conferred on the central bank. Such independence per se may not be expected to have any effect on monetary growth and inflation. Its importance lies in the fact that it can contribute to adoption of a time horizon on the part of a central banks' governing board that is longer in comparison to policy makers who are directly responsible to parliament and subject to volatile electoral influences. Given the potential problem of relatively short time horizons during transition, the creation of institutions that are enabled to adopt a long term view could appear even more important, particularly with regard to the institution controlling base money growth and thus inflation: neither for industrial nor for developing countries is it controversial that inflation inhibits economic growth in the long run. In addition, and as mentioned above, in the long run and on average, unemployment in industrial countries is a positive function of inflation. There has been progress in formalizing central bank independence and in econometrically testing the derived model.[12] Conveying relative independence can be interpreted as a form of commitment which, in turn, influences credibility of a government and central bank. The concept of commitment of governments (sometimes termed 'precommitment') was introduced in economic analysis as a factor crucial in expectations formation. For instance, if a government, whose debt is relatively high, decides to pursue fiscal adjustment associated with indexing this debt, then (to the extent that this latter move is irreversible) it restricts the freedom of action of future governments to use the inflation tax as a means of debt reduction. Consequently, market participants are likely to have lower inflationary expectations with a potential immediate and negative impact on price increases and interest rates. The empirical evidence supports the hypothesis that commitment in form of a central bank's independence is an important variable explaining growth of the monetary base and thus the distribution of inflation. Although measuring independence is inherently limited due to factors which are difficult to quantify or are unobservable, Cukierman's (1992) comprehensive analysis, based on three indices of independence (legal variables derived from central bank laws, turnover rate of central bank governors, and use of the Delphi method) corroborates this hypothesis. Specifically, inflation appears to be negatively affected by both the turnover rate of central bank governors, and the joint contribution of indices of independence on the basis of legal and questionnaire variables. A Granger causality test confirms the expectation for inflation and independence to interact: using the governors turnover rate as a proxy for independence, inflation appears to be positively affected by eroding independence, and independence appears to be eroded by inflation.

The analysis also suggests that a high degree of central bank independence may be important to achieve compliance with legal limitations on central bank credit to the government: in general, it appears that this compliance is rather poor and that inflation is accommodated through central bank credit. This finding is consistent with the above mentioned experience in Poland, where, since 1989, the lending limits do not appear to have been binding.[13] It appears also relevant to note Cukierman's (1992, p. 395) finding that the effective degree of central bank independence declines if, on the one hand, the relative size of the government as a borrower on capital markets increases, and if, on the other hand, the share of marketable government obligations in the central bank's portfolio decreases. The latter influence is due to the fact that if the treasury restricts trading in government securities, the central bank's capability to conduct open market operations is, *ceteris paribus*, inhibited.[14] In sum, these considerations suggest that central bank independence should not be viewed primarily as a question of control of public agencies directly through parliament. A society is likely to raise its welfare if it permits the central bank to operate on the basis of a long term view.

Turning to the 'bad' debt problem in banks' balance sheets, its adverse impact on the evolution of financial systems has two aspects: first, newly established banks are not burdened and therefore equality in competition is, *ceteris paribus*, not given. Second, owing to the economic costs a bank incurs if it would force a borrower into bankruptcy or owing to ineffective bankruptcy laws, banks with 'bad' debt may continue to extend credit to insolvent firms and/or they may capitalize interest due, particularly when a 'bail-out' by the government is expected. If credit continues to be allocated to insolvent firms, society incurs a welfare loss which is twofold: on the one hand, the recipient firms will not be able to serve this debt implying that some members of society will eventually pay it off (including interest and minus the market value of the firm). On the other hand, since credit demand by viable firms has been crowded out, society forsakes the long run return on investments that could have been financed. To prevent continuation of lending to public enterprises that are nonviable in the long run but nevertheless not forced into bankruptcy, these enterprises should be financed through a separate public agency or directly through the budget until a final decision about them is taken. This move would end adding to the stock of 'bad' debt in banks' balance sheets. Steps in this direction have been taken in all considered countries. To eliminate the 'bad' debt, several authors recommended socialization prior to privatization of banks, since this would not alter the income distribution[15] However, socialization bears the danger of overburdening public finance and thus credibility of further debt finance. A preferable approach may be seen in a write-off: banks would cancel 'bad' debt in the amount of deposits held by the respective enterprise. The resulting gap would then be covered by government bonds with long maturity (say 30 years) which could carry relatively low fixed interest so as to minimize the burden on the fiscal balance. The moral hazard problem could thus be contained, equality of banks in competition restored, and the fiscal burden limited.[16] Regarding attainment of adequate own capital ratios of banks, two questions arise: first, may the guidelines established by the BIS or EC be evaluated as appropriate, and second, should capital injections be preferred over granting a period of adjustment? As regards the first question, the BIS rules consider capital adequacy based on credit risk. They may be amended to include risks such as open positions in foreign exchange and term structure (the EC directive on own capital is an adoption of the BIS rules). The risks Eastern European banks are taking by holding loans that were extended at fixed interest rates, while deposit rates are, in principle, flexible, are not covered. In addition, according to the BIS definition of own capital, 'supplementary capital' is permitted to account for 50 per cent of the required ratio of 8 per cent of risk adjusted assets. Government debt on the part of OECD countries is given a risk weight of zero. For two reasons this definition may appear weak: first, the quality of 'supplementary capital' is clearly lower than that of core capital. Second, some OECD governments pay a higher interest rate on bonds of a given maturity than private market participants. The latter fact may indicate that it is problematical to assign debt owed by OECD governments a risk weight of zero. In addition, structural change in financial intermediation, caused, for instance, by financial innovations, implies that regulatory authorities lag behind actual developments in assessing risks taken by banks. Therefore, it may appear preferable to contain the moral hazard problem primarily through reliance on market forces (and thus through relatively high required own capital to asset ratios, where the definition of own capital could correspond to that of 'core' capital in the recommendations concerning banking supervision of the Bank for International Settlements (paid-in capital plus certain reserves).[17]

Regarding the second question as to further capital injections versus granting banks a medium-term adjustment period to attain the required own capital ratio, the former approach would burden public finances whereas the second approach would put pressure on banks to retain earnings (given underdeveloped markets for equity). Since most of those banks who hold the 'bad' debt are still government owned, profits could be ordered to be used for write-offs. However, a reasonable estimate of the adjustment period required to enable 'bad' loans in some Eastern European countries to be written off out of profits could exceed a decade.[18] Thus, in these countries recapitalization could appear unavoidable. A precondition for elimination of non-performing loans to result in improved efficiency of capital allocation is, however, the separation of viable from nonviable public enterprises and bankruptcy law enforcement associated with well defined property rights to provide sources of collateral.

As regards provisioning of deposit insurance, its economic implication (contribution to preventing bank runs and thus panics and liquidity crises) is empirically underpinned: following the introduction of the Banking Act of 1933 in the United States (which became effective in 1934), and whose most important element was government deposit insurance, failures of banks declined precipitously (Fig. 3.1). As a result of the Garn-St Germain Act of 1982, which granted expanded lending and investment powers to savings and loan associations and unitary savings and loan holding companies, and thus permitted the moral hazard problem to materialize, bank failures increased sharply. This rise may not be interpreted as a problem of deposit insurance per se. Rather, the problem consists of inducing banks to take prudent actions and it may appear questionable whether risk related deposit insurance premiums suffice to securing risk-averse bank behaviour. In sum, rapid introduction of deposit insurance may be called for in Eastern European countries and it should be financed through premiums which, ideally, reflect riskiness of the respective institution,[19] but even

129

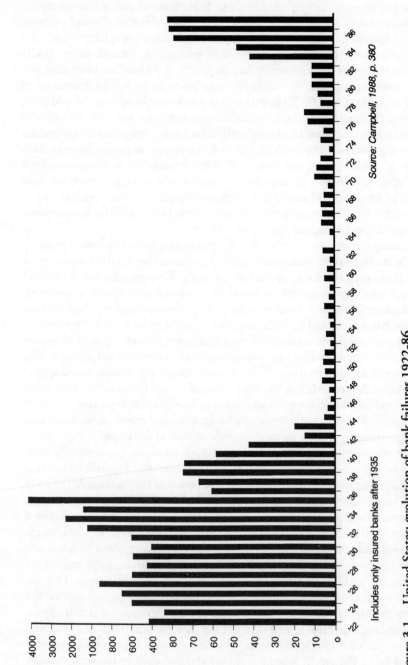

Includes only insured banks after 1935

Figure 3.1   United States: evolution of bank failures 1922-86

under this latter provision its substantial positive externalities could only be expected to materialize if banks are subject to comprehensive prudential regulation including high required own capital ratios.

The fact that Eastern Europe's financial systems are bank-based has implications for both the allocation of capital and efficacy of monetary policy. Turning to the allocation of capital, with equity markets underdeveloped, firms depend mainly on loans for financing during the coming years. Given this fact, it appears possible to derive implications with regard to the allocation of capital, distribution of risk, and firm behaviour.[20] Bank behaviour, in general, and under the conditions of insufficient regulation and macroeconomic instability, in particular, is explained in Appendix II. Here, it is assumed that moral hazard is contained owing to effective supervision of banks (and thus adverse selection and adverse incentive effects are absent, which would cause a newly created loss of output and additions to the existing stock of 'bad' debt). It is also assumed that bankruptcy laws are enforced and property rights defined so that the bank is not deterred from forcing a borrower into bankruptcy if necessary. This latter assumption implies that inter enterprise credit is at a normal level. Then two cases need to be distinguished: if macroeconomic instability prevails, bank lending will consist nearly entirely of short term loans. With stability, both short term and long term loans will constitute the brunt of corporate financing in Eastern Europe. In the first case, the volume of credit, in the aggregate, will be smaller than in the second case, because banks ration relatively more so as to protect themselves and hence also society from losses. In addition, risk sharing between the bank and the borrower is absent with the firm paying a relatively high (real) interest rate. Enterprises are on a 'short leash', since refusal to renew the (short term) loan may mean bankruptcy. Banks effectively control resource allocation and monitor managers. Firm behaviour, in turn, will be relatively risk averse so as to comply with banks' demands. Macroeconomic growth is likely to be inhibited, because risk taking is effectively rationed out. In the second case, where macroeconomic stability prevails, firms receive both short term and long term loans. Time horizons are relatively long and risk sharing between the bank and borrower occurs so as to establish long term relationships and economize on information costs. Credit rationing would be less stringent. Consequently, managers, who are also enabled to take a long run view, can afford to increase risk taking (since the real interest rate is lower than under macroeconomic instability and because they are granted more freedom of action). The economy is likely to be lifted on a higher growth path (less so than in the case where equity financing was readily available). In both cases, however, banks exert considerable influence in the economy, probably more than the owners (as discussed below), because firms depend on loans. If owners have superior information as regards the markets in which their firms operate, society would pay a price in form of lost growth due to insufficient equity markets. As regards the distribution of risk, a dominance of loans means that risk is not shared with the provider of capital.

Society on the whole bears less risk, which is reflected in lower growth.

The consequences for monetary policy of a bank-based financial system under liberalized interest rates with underdeveloped securities markets are given by reliance on reserve requirements and the discount rate to control the money supply. Since these instruments are crude measures relative to open market operations, control of the money supply is rendered more difficult. In addition, even if the central bank is granted control over its asset side, control of the money supply is impaired through disintermediation of credit flows, such as significant inter-enterprise lending, currency substitution, and subsidized credit. Appendix II considers the first and second problem and suggests to raise reserve requirements on foreign currency holdings. Subsidized credit concerns mainly housing to improving labour mobility and thus poses the problem of trading off its potential benefits in terms of reduced unemployment against its costs in terms of the burden for the fiscal balance and impaired efficacy of monetary policy. This points to the need to review subsidies periodically.

Finally, turning to the issue of the evolving enterprise ownership structure, it appears helpful to adopt the theoretical distinction between an 'insider-' or 'bank-based control system' versus an 'outsider-' or 'stock market control system'. The former characterizes an ownership structure where voting rights are dominantly exercised by institutions such as financial intermediaries who may possess superior information and could thus credibly control managers of non-financial enterprises (also by taking seats on the boards of firms). In the latter system, voting rights are exercised by individual share owners who may hold relatively small amounts of shares. The question is which system would better serve to oversee the enterprise sector. Both systems have advantages and disadvantages. The major disadvantage of the former lies in its potential to jeopardize competition (e.g., a bank exercises voting rights so as to promote concentration or collusion in order to raise profits). The major disadvantage of the latter is given by a potential lack of interest on the part of shareholders to exercise voting rights. Control of enterprises may thus be insufficient or exerted by minority shareholders such as banks (or pension funds, mutual funds, or insurance companies), or it may be indirectly exerted by other firms, namely through the threat of a potential take-over since firms are continuously up for auction. Theoretical analysis of these stylized systems may not be sufficient to derive a recommendation for Eastern Europe. Empirical analysis may be crucial. The former system, subject to significant qualifications, dominates in most industrial countries, whereas the second system, also subject to qualifications, prevails in the United States and the United Kingdom. A universal banking system, where banks are permitted both to hold equity and exercise voting rights for depositors of shares, may have advantages compared to a system where corporate control is achieved indirectly through the threat of take-overs. There is no firm empirical evidence corroborating this hypothesis. However, the spate of take-overs witnessed in the United States over the past decade, sometimes financed through issuance of high risk bonds, may have contributed to a short-ening of time horizons (Corbett and Mayer, 1991). This (potential) effect cannot be evaluated as (constraint) Pareto efficient. By contrast, a system where banks are permitted to control nonfinancial enterprises either through equity holdings or through exercising voting rights in lieu of the owner, contributes, *ceteris paribus*, to effective control and long time horizons, because banks can be expected to have superior knowledge about firms. In addition, the relationships between firms and banks could be relatively stable. The main potential danger posed by the dominance of banks, concentration and collusion, would require enforcement of anti-trust regulation and open borders for trade. It thus could appear that the bank-based capital markets in Eastern Europe and dispersed ownership of corporate equity are not to the disadvantage of effective control of managers, provided banks would be permitted to acquire equity and to exercise voting rights in lieu of depositors of shares.

To summarize, to improve the efficiency of capital allocation may call for a separation of nonviable public enterprises from those that will be privatized, a write-off of 'bad' debt in banks' balance sheets or – in countries where this problem may not be solvable through a write-off – a final recapitalization of banks, improvement of banking regulation so as to compensate for deficiencies in BIS standards and to prevent moral hazard from materializing, a phasing out of subsidized credit, introduction of deposit insurance, and improvement of the effective degree of central bank independence and efficacy of central bank oper-ations. Within this system, bank lending is likely to dominate resulting in tight control of enterprises through banks which would be reinforced if the latter are permitted to hold equity and to exercise voting rights in lieu of depositors of shares. This may be expected to provide for effective control of non-financial enterprises and could promote relatively long time horizons. To prevent poten-tial adverse effects on growth, enforcement of anti-trust regulation and open borders for trade would be required. The present structure of segmentation of the banking systems by sector and geographical area is not appropriate. Banks should compete nation-wide as universal banks. If inflation was expected to be relatively high, increased credit rationing would occur, provided banking regu-lation is effective. If inflation is moderate, credit rationing will be less severe, permitting increased risk taking on the part of non-financial enterprises and thus somewhat higher growth. Several channels through which inflation impairs the function of financial intermediaries in allocating resources have become evident. Finally, it could appear preferable for policies to concentrate on these basic aspects of financial system reform rather than to attempt to com-plete financial markets as, for instance, through futures markets.

Given the importance of macroeconomic stability for efficient financial intermediation, the following section examines the magnitude of fiscal adjust-ment that could be called for so as to reduce inflation and inflationary expectations.

Notes

1   This does not imply that fixing the rate of savings enables policy-makers to determine the rate of growth: on the contrary, prior to transition, Eastern European countries exhibited relatively high aggregate savings ratios associated with poor economic growth. Poor allocation of capital (besides missing incentives for work effort) provides a major explanation.

2   In Eastern European countries savings and lending institutions were separate.

3   Parallel markets for foreign currency existed in Eastern European countries but there were no informal markets for loans and securities.

4   These risks are: credit risk, price risk, market-liquidity risk, term-structure risk, currency risk, and transfer risk.

5   There are two major reasons for this: first, privatization requires time, and second, dividend payments may thus be contained so as to facilitate a write-off of 'bad' debt.

6   For an analysis of these experiences, see Villanueva and Mirakhor, 1990.

7   A complication would arise in the absence of debt socialization, namely the potential crowding out of these banks through banks not burdened by 'bad' debt since the latter are, *ceteris paribus*, more competitive. The bad debt problem is evaluated in Section 4.

8   In Romania, it may have been known to the public that the problem of rising inter-enterprise arrears re-emerged after an initial stock adjustment during the second year of transition. The proposed bankruptcy law had not been passed by parliament. In Bulgaria, the public may be aware of the problem of high external public debt relative to the other considered Eastern European countries. (At end of 1992 total net public debt is estimated at about 140 per cent of GDP). In addition, as mentioned above, both countries did not grant relative independence to their central banks.

9   For an overview of principal features of the exemplary regulation of primary and secondary securities markets in the United States, see Campbell, 1988, pp. 345-368). The seminal article on regulation of securities markets is Stigler, 1965.

10 There is dissension as to the contribution of this type of financial intermediation to society's welfare. Specifically, it is questioned whether all resources used in securities and foreign exchange markets are welfare increasing. This criticism can be traced back to Keynes' apprehension concerning the rationality of securities markets which found support by others such as Tobin, 1978, 1984, and Stiglitz, 1989. Tobin favours a tax on certain transactions in markets for foreign exchange which, in his view, could be expected to reduce speculation. The taxation of transactions on securities markets may, however, be problematic, because speculation can be welfare increasing. In addition, as described in Appendix I, some types of securities and economic activity that are subject to strongest criticism have

largely been absent in financial systems characterized by universal banking.

11 It may be noted that Germany, whose corporate securities markets remained underdeveloped since the Second World War, recently established an agency overseeing and regulating the securities market and tightened legislation on insider trading.

12 As noted above, it may be reasonable to assume a central bank, who is granted relative independence, to adopt a lower rate of time preference than treasury officials whose objectives may be subject to more volatile shifts. (Cukierman, 1992 pp. 351-368)) assumes that both institutions maximize the expected present value of their objectives. It is assumed that the central bank applies a larger discount factor (denoted β_{CB}) than the latter (denoted β_G) : $\beta_{CB} > \beta_G$. Since only one rate of time preference can be applied to objectives intended to be attained through monetary growth (e.g. an employment target, an inflation rate), this rate may be written as a weighted average of the preferences of the government and of the central bank:

$\beta = \alpha \beta_G + (1 - \alpha) \beta_{CB}$ where α is the weight given to government preferences $(0 < \alpha < 1)$. Hence, the higher the degree of independence of the central bank, the smaller will be α, and thus the larger will be the overall discount factor applied to the objective function in which inflation is the argument: $\delta\beta/\delta\alpha < 0$. Identical objective functions of the treasury and the central bank are assumed of the form:

$$\max \; E_{G_{t=0}} \sum_{t=0}^{\infty} \beta^t \left[(m_t - E_{MP}[m_t \mid I_t]) \, x_t - \frac{m_t^2}{2} \right]$$

where m_t is the inflation rate in period t, E_t is the expectations operator conditional on information sets available in period t where the subscript G denotes either the treasury or the central bank, and subscript MP denotes other market participants, I_t is the information set available to the latter in period t, x_t is a coefficient indicating policy makers concern about higher than natural unemployment, and β is given as noted above. Cukierman obtains two important results: the mean and variance of inflation will be higher the lower is the degree of independence of the central bank as measured by the variable α. It is also noteworthy that this model with its definition of independence can explain positive cross country correlation of the mean and variance of inflation.

13 Lending limits specified in terms of government's expenditures or revenues appear to be relatively accommodative in comparison with absolute cash limits. Eastern European central bank laws specify limits in terms of revenues or expenditures: in Bulgaria and in the Czech and Slovak Republics the limit was set at 5 per cent of revenues collected in the previous year; in Hungary the limit was set at 3 per cent (starting in 1995) of revenues

expected for the current fiscal year, in Poland and in Romania, the criterion expenditures applies, with the limits set at 2 per cent of projected current annual expenditures in Poland, and 10 per cent in Romania.

14 An additional limitation of independence could arise if the central bank, through subsidized credit, assumes the function of a development bank.

15 Calvo and Frenkel (1991) emphasized debt socialization prior to privatization, since this may be expected to contribute to a reduced risk of moral hazard arising in the post-privatization era. Brainard (1991) also emphasized debt socialization whose effectiveness requires, however, simultaneous implementation of structural reform measures (i.e. adoption of Western accounting principles and prudential supervision).

16 The approach is analysed in Dornbusch and Wolf, 1990.

17 This definition of capital would facilitate the assessment of banks' creditworthiness and thus promote transparency of the banking market. A narrow definition of banks' own capital may, *ceteris paribus*, contain risk-taking on the part of banks, because it would be more difficult for the bank to conceal a loss. The major disadvantage of a narrow definition is that the risk for bank runs to occur could increase. However, deposit insurance would tend to reduce this risk.

18 Table 4.2 presents estimates as a share of GDP of this burden.

19 Establishment of credit rating agencies could facilitate such pricing.

20 Both, equity financing and loans have distinct advantages and disadvantages. In Section 2, the beneficial aspects of equity financing from a social welfare point of view were emphasized: *ceteris paribus*, an economy may experience a higher growth path which is less volatile if equity financing dominates and if management is controlled such that it acts in the interest of shareholders. This is because entrepreneurs have enhanced discretion since risk is shared with the investor. They do not 'have their backs to the wall' (as may be the case with debt financing, even if it is subject to implicit contracts and thus risk sharing).

4 Sustainability of fiscal policy

1. The problem

Eastern European countries entered the period of transition with widely differing total public net debt to GDP ratios. Questions that arise are whether the countries could 'afford' increases in the respective ratio in the sense that adverse effects on economic growth and destabilizing reactions are unlikely. In addition, if an increase is prevented owing to inflationary financing of the deficit, it may be asked whether this would offer a viable alternative to a rising debt to GDP ratio. These questions thus concern the aspect of sustainability of fiscal deficits, which, in turn, concentrates on the implications of an existing debt stock and, inter alia, the Government need to recourse to additional tax measures, increases in revenues from seignorage, or spending reductions. In concentrating on this aspect, this section does not consider other important issues pertaining to fiscal policy, namely the preferable means to raise revenues during transition until the shares of VATs and income taxes in total revenues have risen to satisfactory levels, and the distortions created by fiscal policy on investment, saving, and the labour market (issue of distortionary effects of fiscal policy). However, the issue of sustainability is often analysed excluding the effects of fiscal policy on aggregate demand and savings (the fiscal impact and final effects of fiscal policy), although the question as to whether fiscal deficits affect private savings behaviour appears to be central in an analysis of sustainability. Hence, the assessment in Section 3 considers these effects.

The literature on public debt in general, and on the issue of sustainability in particular, grew extensively during the 1970s and particularly the 1980s and early 1990s in response to the increased significance of the problem. While the major contributions during the 1960s and 1970s concentrated on the pure theory of public debt (e.g. Tobin, 1963; Barro, 1974, 1979; Blinder and Solow, 1974), research during the 1980s and early 1990s provided both major theoretical contributions (e.g. Sargent and Wallace, 1981; Buiter, 1983, 1985; Eisner and Peiper, 1984; Feldstein, 1985; Masson, 1985; Stiglitz, 1986; Bispham, 1987; Spaventa, 1987; Hansson and Stuart, 1987; Leiderman and Blejer, 1988; Calvo, 1988) and contributions directed toward developing new indicators of the above mentioned main aspects of fiscal policy, in particular the aspect of sustainability (e.g. Zee, 1988; Kotlikoff, 1989; Blanchard, 1990; Blanchard et. al., 1990; Chouraqui et. al., 1990; Horne, 1991). In two relatively recent contributions the analysis of sustainability was carried further, departing from concentrating on the intertemporal budget constraint: Alesina and Drazen (1989) address the question as to why fiscal adjustments that are known to eventually have to be adopted are usually delayed. By explicitly modelling distributional conflict they show that the expected timing of stabilization is a function of economic and political characteristics of a country.[1] Drazen and Helpman (1990) study the case where an unbounded present value of government debt and hence budget deficits that are known to be not feasible in the long run, induce expectations of a future policy change. They show how such expectations induce fluctuations in the rate of inflation that seem to be unrelated to the budget deficit. Hence, uncertainty about the timing and nature of a policy switch can have significant adverse effects on macroeconomic variables.

The contribution by Zee (1988) provided a neo-classical, overlapping generations' model that is solvable for an optimal debt to GNP ratio. Depending on the parameter values, the optimal debt to GNP ratio can be positive or negative. Provided reasonable estimates of the parameter values would be obtainable, it may be possible to implement his model empirically.

On the other hand, the empirical evidence may suggest that the search for a critical public debt to GNP or GDP ratio, beyond which financial instability arises, causing a drastic remedy to the original problem by diminishing the real value of debt, could be fruitless.[2] Therefore, the following assessment of sustainability of fiscal policy focuses on the government's intertemporal budget constraint. It should be noted, however, that the latter appears to be a rather weak criterion of sustainability, because calculating, for instance, a rise in taxation required for a government to be able to meet its expenditure goals, leaves out the question as to whether society would tolerate this rise (Appendix III).

2. Illustrative calculations

Table 4.1 presents estimates of domestic and external debt to GDP ratios in the considered Eastern European countries. Knowledge of these ratios is required in performing calculations showing whether the present level of taxation appears sufficient to hold the debt to GDP ratio constant during a given time horizon and to maintain solvency of the government. Analysis of the sustainability aspect of fiscal policy needs to concentrate on the total public sector, since a

138

Table 4.1
Selected Eastern European countries:
estimates of net domestic and net external public debt 1991-92*

(As per cent of GDP; end period)

	1991	1992
	Net Domestic Public Debt	
Bulgaria	14	14
Czech Republic	5	7
Hungary	9	17
Poland	11	16
Romania	—	—
Slovak Republic	9	15
	Net External Public Debt	
Bulgaria	190	125
Czech Republic	—	15
Hungary	57	51
Poland	59	61
Romania	10	15
Slovak Republic	—	26
	Total Net Public Debt	
Bulgaria	204	138
Czech Republic	—	21
Hungary	67	68
Poland	70	77
Romania	10	16
Slovak Republic	—	41

Source: International Monetary Fund, Data Fund.

* Discrepancies due to rounding.

deficit in an off-budget account poses the same burden for the taxpayer as does the fiscal deficit of the central government. Consequently, the debt measures are comprehensive in the sense that they comprise the state budget, local authorities, social security, special public funds, and other extra-budgetary accounts. The net domestic public debt ratios were obtained by adding the stock of outstanding government bonds (in countries where these have been issued) to the stock of outstanding net credit owed by the general government sector to the banking system. The latter figure was adjusted so as to prevent double counting of external debt, which, however, raises uncertainties in some cases related to the quality of data. A further qualification is given by the fact that privatization is likely to cause deposits held by governments to become more volatile resulting, *ceteris paribus*, in volatility of the net debt to GDP ratios. Given these limitations, Table 4.1 shows that during 1992, net domestic public debt as a share of GDP rose considerably in Hungary, Poland, and the Slovak Republic. Despite fiscal deficits and output declines in all countries, Romania and

Bulgaria prevented a rise in the debt ratio through inflation. In Romania, net domestic public debt became slightly positive. In general, the ratios appear relatively moderate. Net external public debt ratios were obtained by deducting official foreign exchange reserves from gross external debt.[3] These ratios are also subject to a significant margin of error, because part of this debt may become private owing to privatization. For instance, in the former Czech and Slovak Federal Republic, at end-1992 about 21 per cent of external debt pertained to public non-financial enterprises, and about 38 per cent to banks. However, for the purpose of the following calculations, the assumption is made that all external debt falls on the public. Hence, with respect to the applied debt to GDP ratios, the calculations can be considered a 'worst-case' scenario, based on the rationale that a government who maximizes welfare of its citizens will be risk averse, and thus set up its fiscal plan using conservative estimates. Table 4.1 does not comprise payments arrears among public enterprises and nonperforming loans in banks' balance sheets. Although the margin of error regarding these debts is large, estimates are available and therefore it appears preferable to consider this burden. Table 4.2 presents the estimates: regarding inter-enterprise arrears, in Hungary, the Central Bank evaluates so-called 'involuntary inter enterprise' lending, which stood at about 6 per cent of GDP in mid-1992 and declined subsequently, perhaps related to the increased number of bankruptcies. An estimate of 5 per cent is shown as a conservative proxy for a potential burden for public finance. It was also applied to Poland and to the Czech and Slovak Republics.[4] Regarding Bulgaria and Romania, estimates of inter enterprise arrears differ (ranging from about 10 to 20 per cent of GDP at end-1992). A potential burden of 10 per cent is shown in Table 4.4 for both countries.

Estimates of the shares of non-performing loans in banks' balance sheets concerning end-1991 are also presented: their corresponding GDP shares range from 7 per cent in Poland to 24 per cent in Romania. Regarding the Czech and Slovak Republics the estimates which apply to the former Czech and Slovak Republic are shown for both countries. For the purpose of the calculations, estimates of nonperforming loans were added to the net domestic public debt ratios shown in Table 4.1. Inter-enterprise arrears were not considered. The resulting estimated total net public debt to GDP ratios range from about 35 per cent in the Czech Republic to about 156 per cent in Bulgaria.

On the basis of these ratios, illustrative calculations are performed, using the 'budget gap-' and 'forward looking balance sheet' approach (Appendix IV)[5] Different discount rates to outstanding debt and primary balances are applied in an attempt to assess the sustainability of current and expected primary fiscal balances. The budget gap approach is based on the definition of sustainability provided by Blanchard (1990), namely stabilization of the debt to GDP ratio within a certain time horizon. Here, importance is attached to the fact that this definition excludes inflation as a means to alleviate the public debt burden, giving rise to the following question: is it conceivable that under conservative estimates

Table 4.2
Selected Eastern European countries:
estimates of inter-enterprise arrears and
'bad' debt in banks' balance sheets *

(As per cent of GDP unless otherwise indicated; end period)

	1992
	Estimates of inter-enterprise arrears
Bulgaria	10
Czech Republic	5
Hungary	5
Poland	5
Romania	10
Slovak Republic	5

	Estimates of non-performing loans in banks' balance sheets at end-1991	
	as per cent of credit to non-financial enterprises	*as per cent of GDP*
Bulgaria	40	17
Czech Republic	20	13
Hungary	20	8
Poland	30	7
Romania	20	24
Slovak Republic	20	13

	Net domestic public debt (including estimated 'bad' debt in banks' balance sheets)
Bulgaria	31
Czech Republic	20
Hungary	25
Poland	23
Romania	24
Slovak Republic	28

	Total net public debt (including estimate of net external public debt)
Bulgaria	156
Czech Republic	35
Hungary	76
Poland	84
Romania	39
Slovak Republic	54

Source: International Monetary Fund, Data Fund.

* Discrepancies due to rounding.

of the future path of non-interest expenditures and revenues, Eastern European governments service public debt, including the burden that would result from a recapitalization of banks, without resorting to inflation and thus paying a positive ex-post real interest rate? Specifically, a time horizon until 1996 is adopted. Total government revenues and non-interest expenditures as a share of GDP are exogenous and forecast on the basis of recent developments. Real GDP growth is also exogenous.[6] It is assumed that banks are recapitalized. Hence, the total net public debt to GDP ratios shown in Table 4.2 are applied. Further assumptions are, first, governments announce stabilization of the form that the planned path of primary balances, which are surpluses except in Hungary, will be adhered to. This could be achieved through expenditure growth less than expected output growth and, if necessary, temporary fees levied on government services for several years until the VATs and income taxes yield revenues whose relative size would be comparable to that in industrial countries;[7] second, relative independence is conferred on central banks whose objective function contains only the inflation rate; third, price levels are held constant during 1994 through 1996 and elimination of inflation does not affect the growth forecasts; fourth, the monetary base grows by the same rate as real output. Under these restrictive assumptions, equation (1) (Appendix III) is used to solve for that critical (real) interest rate which each country could afford to pay on its total net debt (including external debt) without causing the debt to GDP ratio to change during 1994-96. These critical interest rates are approximately 5 per cent in Bulgaria, 3.5 per cent in Hungary, and 6 per cent in Poland and Romania. The scenario thus shows that under restrictive assumptions and using reasonable estimates of primary fiscal balances, positive real interest rates are compatible with stabilization of the debt to GDP ratios. It follows that even if Eastern European countries would decide to eliminate the distortions created by nonperforming loans in banks' balance sheets (moral hazard, capitalization of interest, crowding out of credit to viable enterprises, inequities in competition) through recapitalization and thus a further increase in public debt, the debt burden could appear to be manageable without resorting to inflation. *ceteris paribus*, fiscal deficits would decline, because, first, rising output growth rates provide for a decrease of the difference between the interest rate and output growth rate and, second, an increasing share of the deficits would be financed through seignorage due to growth in *real* base money. Hence, borrowing requirements decline.[8] Provided inflation abates, the second effect is likely to be reinforced through growth of demand for real money balances in excess of output growth.

One year budgetary gaps are calculated on the basis of equation (9) (Appendix IV). Regarding the illustrative non-inflation scenarios for the years 1994-96, the gaps would be zero if exactly the critical interest rate was shown under which the debt to GDP ratio would remain constant.[9] Regarding 1993, this indicator is strongly negative, because the expected actual (highly negative) real interest rates are used and hence all countries may experience a decline in the debt to GDP ratios.[10] In addition to the non-inflation scenarios for the years 1994-96, which take the expected development during 1993 as given, a medium-term budgetary gap is calculated, assuming that it may be a policy goal to achieve positive ex-post real interest rates even during 1993, so as to promote savings. These medium-term budgetary gaps (based on equation (8), Appendix IV) indicate the (permanent, i.e., annual) adjustment that would be required for the debt to GDP ratios at the end of the forecast period (1996) to be the same as those at end-1992. Since a government does not face a solvency constraint if the interest rate is below the rate of output growth and given that it should not be assumed to set up its fiscal plan under this condition (Appendix III), a real interest rate on total debt of 5 per cent is applied[11] and the expected average growth rate during 1993-96. To stabilize the estimated end-1992 debt to GDP ratios under these conditions with the path of expenditures and revenues given as shown in the Table, substantial adjustment would be required, particularly in Bulgaria and Hungary.[12] Such calculations are relatively sensitive to changes in the parameters.[13] If Eastern European countries continue to experience negative ex-post real interest rates on public debt or even slightly positive rates of up to about 2 per cent, the forecast primary balances as shown in Table 4.3 would suffice to stabilize present debt to GDP ratios in the medium-term. The question is, however, whether economic growth would be higher, if inflation was prevented due to fiscal adjustment.

Table 4.4 presents calculations on the basis of the 'forward looking balance sheet' approach (Appendix IV) which are similar to those performed above, because the definition of government assets and hence revenues is the same.[14] However, for the purpose of illustration, the net debt to GDP ratios at end 1992, excluding the potential burden resulting from a recapitalization of banks, are applied. In addition, in light of the remark made above, that an assumed real interest rate of 5 per cent could be rather low, a discount rate of 5 per cent (consistent with an estimated real return on capital of about 7-10 per cent and growth of about 3-5 per cent) is applied. Subtracting estimated total net public debt from the present values of expected primary balances yields an estimate of the respective Government's net worth. As shown in Table 4.4a, under these assumptions only the Government of the Czech Republic would appear to be solvent, or, in other words, meet ex-ante its intertemporal budget constraint. Provided Bulgaria's relatively high present primary surplus could be assumed to be expected by markets to prevail, its public sector would be solvent if a discount rate of 2 per cent was applicable (Table 4.4a). The same is true in the case of Romania, because here the debt ratio is relatively low. However, it needs to be noted that the risk premium governments pay, and thus also the total interest burden, depends on both the expectation of market participants as to primary balances and the discount rate they apply.[15] Hence, a government that is perceived to be insolvent has the option to lower its debt servicing burden and to restore solvency, if it can convince markets that its future primary surpluses rise sufficiently.

143

Table 4.3
Selected Eastern European countries: illustrative debt sustainability scenarios

	1989	1990	1991	1992	1993	1994	1995	1996
(As percent of GDP except interest rate and GDP growth rate which are in percent; stock variables are end of period figures)								
Bulgaria								
Revenues	57.9	52.5	39.3	36.3	34.6	35.0	35.0	35.0
Expenditures	61.4	65.1	54.1	45.3	40.9	39.2	39.2	39.2
Non-interest expend.	58.4	56.1	36.7	39.0	32.0	32.0	32.0	32.0
Real interest rate	—	—	—	—	-12.0	5.0	5.0	5.0
Real GDP growth rate	2.0	-11.8	-23.3	-8.1	—	1.3	2.7	3.5
Primary balance	-0.5	-3.6	2.6	-2.6	2.6	3.0	3.0	3.0
Annual budgetary gap	—	—	—	—	-3.0	2.4	0.4	-0.8
Medium-term budg. gap	—	—	—	—	—	1.6	—	—
Total net debt stock	—	—	—	156.0	145.3	147.7	148.1	147.3
Monetary base	—	—	—	12.4	11.7	11.7	11.7	11.7
Fiscal balance	-3.5	-12.6	-14.8	-9.0	-6.4	-4.2	-4.2	-4.2
Seignorage (unadjusted)	—	—	—	—	4.4	0.1	0.3	0.4
Hungary								
Revenues	59.6	57.4	58.1	55.2	56.8	57.8	57.8	57.8
Expenditures	60.9	57.0	58.8	63.4	63.5	61.6	61.6	61.6
Non-interest expend.	58.4	53.8	55.4	58.7	58.7	58.7	58.7	58.7
Real interest rate	—	—	—	—	-6.0	3.5	3.5	3.5
Real GDP growth rate	-0.2	-4.3	-10.2	-5.0	1.5	3.5	4.5	5.0
Primary balance	1.1	3.6	2.7	-3.5	-1.9	-0.9	-0.9	-0.9
Annual budgetary gap	—	—	—	—	-2.1	0.9	0.2	-0.2
Medium-term budg. gap	—	—	—	—	—	2.0	—	—
Total net debt stock	—	—	—	76.0	74.2	75.1	75.3	75.0
Monetary base	—	—	—	33.3	31.3	31.3	31.3	31.3
Fiscal balance	-1.3	0.4	-0.7	-8.2	-6.7	-3.4	-3.4	-3.4
Seignorage (unadjusted)	—	—	—	—	2.8	1.1	1.4	1.5
Poland								
Revenues	30.8	33.3	25.8	26.3	25.8	26.0	26.0	26.0
Expenditures	36.9	32.7	32.1	33.7	30.6	29.7	29.7	29.7
Non-interest expend.	36.9	32.3	30.5	30.4	26.9	25.0	25.0	25.0
Real interest rate	—	—	—	—	-15.0	6.0	6.0	6.0
Real GDP growth rate	0.2	-11.6	-7.2	0.8	2.0	4.0	5.0	5.0
Primary balance	-6.1	1.0	-4.7	-4.1	-1.1	1.0	1.0	1.0
Annual budgetary gap	—	—	—	—	-6.3	0.6	-0.2	-0.2
Medium-term budg. gap	—	—	—	—	—	-0.5	—	—
Total net debt stock	—	—	—	84.0	81.2	81.8	81.6	81.4
Monetary base	—	—	—	12.4	11.1	11.1	11.1	11.1
Fiscal balance	-6.1	0.7	-6.3	-7.5	-4.8	-3.7	-3.7	-3.7
Seignorage (unadjusted)	—	—	—	—	2.3	0.4	0.5	0.5
Romania								
Revenues	51.1	37.7	34.3	35.7	33.7	35.2	35.7	35.7
Expenditures	42.7	37.6	35.4	37.6	36.4	36.3	36.4	36.4
Non-interest expend.	42.6	37.5	35.3	37.5	35.0	35.0	35.0	35.0
Real interest rate	—	—	—	—	-50.0	6.0	6.0	6.0
Real GDP growth rate	-5.8	-7.4	-13.7	-10.0	—	2.5	3.0	3.5
Primary balance	8.5	0.2	-0.9	-1.8	-1.3	0.2	0.7	0.7
Annual budgetary gap	—	—	—	—	-16.3	0.6	—	-0.1
Medium-term budg. gap	—	—	—	—	—	1.3	—	—
Total net debt stock	—	—	—	39.0	22.7	23.3	23.3	23.2
Monetary base	—	—	—	9.0	10.5	10.5	10.5	10.5
Fiscal balance	8.4	0.1	-1.0	-1.9	-2.7	-1.1	-0.7	-0.7
Seignorage (unadjusted)	—	—	—	—	5.6	0.3	0.3	0.4

Sources: International Monetary Fund, Data Fund; IMF staff estimates; author.

144

Table 4.4
Selected Eastern European countries:
illustrative calculations of governments' net worths

	Expected primary surplus or deficit(-)	Forecast long-run rate of output growth	Discount rate	Present value of primary balance	Total net public debt (end of 1992)	Govt's net worth
	(As per cent of GDP except output growth rate and discount rate which are in percent)					
Bulgaria	3.0	3.0	5.0	60.0	138.0	-78
Czech Republic	2.0	5.0	5.0	40.0	21.0	19
Hungary	-0.9	4.0	5.0	-18.0	68.0	-86
Poland	1.0	5.0	5.0	20.0	77.0	-57
Romania	0.7	3.0	5.0	14.0	16.0	-2

Sources: International Monetary Fund, staff estimates; author.

Table 4.4a
Selected Eastern European countries:
required primary fiscal surplus to service outstanding public debt

	Assuming discount rate of 2 percent	Assuming discount rate of 5 percent
	(As percent of GDP)	
Bulgaria	2.8	6.9
Czech Republic	0.5	1.1
Hungary	1.4	3.4
Poland	1.5	3.9
Romania	0.3	0.8

Source: Author.

3. Policy considerations

As noted above, it appears difficult to derive empirically an optimal public debt to GDP ratio. For this reason, the concept of stabilization of the ratio was proposed. Stabilization may, however, appear unacceptable if it is achieved by means of inflation, because the latter's adverse effects on welfare are not ascertainable: skewed income distribution is promoted which appears to be opposed to the social values appreciated by Eastern European societies; time horizons are likely to shorten; positive covariance with respect to the returns on investment projects arises which increases both the systemic risk in the economy and the probability of output losses if moral hazard on the part of banks is not prevented from materializing (Appendix II); the increase in systemic risk is likely to have an adverse impact on investment in general, and capital inflows in particular; under a fixed exchange rate system, competitiveness of the economy will deteriorate, under a flexible exchange rate system, it is likely to deteriorate if expectations of depreciation lessen pressure on firms to improve productivity; the function of domestic currency as a store of value deteriorates so that money demand becomes unstable and currency substitution is promoted which, in turn, reduces the tax base of inflation and is likely to have an adverse impact on private savings; tax revenues may also decline owing to lags in collection which is amplified if the collection process cannot be regarded efficient. Moreover, in the long run, inflation cannot reduce the external debt to GDP ratio, because eventually the exchange rate has to be adjusted so as to satisfy purchasing power parity: relatively high inflation is likely to aggravate the external debt burden, because competitiveness and thus the trade balance may deteriorate. Hence, *ceteris paribus*, the external debt burden could call for a constant price level. Table 4.1 showed that in Eastern European countries it is generally external debt that accounts for the most part of net public debt. The domestic net debt to GDP ratios may appear relatively moderate, even if the potential burden of recapitalization of banks is considered. For these reasons, one scenario presented in the previous section concentrated on the case where inflation is prevented as does the following discussion. It focuses on domestic debt because the problem of external debt is identical with that of the economy's competitiveness.

Feldstein (1985) showed that under the condition of full employment (so as to rule out demand effects of fiscal policy), the excess burden associated with financing a temporary increase in government spending is likely to be lower when it is financed through taxing rather than borrowing.[16] The parameter in his model which, *ceteris paribus*, favours tax financing over borrowing, if its value rises, is the market interest rate. Parameters which, *ceteris paribus*, favour borrowing, if their values increase, are the discount rate appropriate in calculating the present value of future annual debt finance burdens, the compensated labour supply elasticity, and the ratio of the government spending increase to the total tax base. Overstating the value of the former parameter and understating the value of the latter ones, it is shown that the excess burden of tax finance is smaller than that of borrowing if the market interest rate is above the appropriate discount rate. Since it is plausible to assume the market interest rate to exceed the appropriate discount rate (due to a tax on interest income or due to the choice of the long run growth rate of real per capita consumption as a proxy for the discount rate when adopting a utilitarian analysis), this finding suggests that taxation is more efficient than borrowing. Taxation is likely to reduce consumption by more than borrowing which would be crucial in the context of Eastern Europe where the physical capital stock is likely to be below its optimal level. If this finding would hold in practice then it would mean, *ceteris paribus*, that increases in government borrowing reduce the capital stock, confirming the arguments of a large earlier literature (e.g., Modigliani, 1961). However, the finding rests on the assumption that fiscal policy does not affect private savings behaviour. If private savings rise so as to offset the impact on national savings of fiscal deficits, then the latter may not adversely affect interest rates and the capital stock. In Eastern European countries private savings ratios rose generally considerably. The question is whether this rise may be attributable to the generally relatively large fiscal deficits since 1991. Barro (1989) provides empirical evidence which supports the hypothesis that private households' demand for goods depends on the expected present value of taxes. However, there are two important exceptions: that of the United States during the 1980s and that of Germany during the entire post World War II period. In these cases the external current account balance was highly positively correlated with the fiscal balance.

In a model where the government maximizes the (strictly concave) utility function of the average market participant (utility being assumed to depend only on growth), it may be reasonable to hypothesize that the government behaves risk-averse in the sense that it considers a potential adverse impact of fiscal deficits on national savings with the resulting burden for capital formation and growth (and in the sense that it uses 'conservative' estimates of revenues and expenditures when setting up its fiscal plan so as to minimize the risk of incurring potentially harmful fiscal deficits). From this perspective, it may follow that, unless there are exceptional circumstances, containment of the net public domestic debt to GDP ratio is imperative. Whether the situation of Eastern Europe should be regarded to be an exception may appear questionable if one considers that capital formation, and thus a rapid rise of the capital-labour ratio, appears to be a precondition for economic growth of the magnitude required to reduce present unemployment rates over the medium term to levels that would be acceptable. From this it may follow that – at least during transition – stabilization of the net domestic public debt to GDP ratio could be regarded as a policy goal of a government that maximizes welfare of its citizens. If, concomitantly, inflation would be contained at a level below that prevailing, on average, in the main competitor countries, the external debt burden would, *ceteris paribus*, decrease which could have, *ceteris paribus*, a positive impact on capital inflows.

Provided the interest rate on total net public debt exceeds the economy's output growth rate, a fiscal deficit, whose non-interest surplus (adjusted for revenue from seignorage) is larger than (equals) the product of interest payments (adjusted for output growth) and the debt to GDP ratio, will result in a declining (stable) debt to GDP ratio. Under the above reasoning and given that achievement of ex-post real interest rates may be regarded to be a policy goal (due to the promotion of both private savings and efficient capital allocation), an upper bound for fiscal deficits sustainable in the medium term would be suggested: it is that deficit which one obtains if the primary surplus is large enough to offset the positive impact of debt interest payments on growth of net debt, and where the revenue component of this deficit in form of seignorage consists of increases in the monetary base which result from increases in desired real money balances due to real output growth. These fiscal deficits were calculated

147

in the illustrative calculations shown in Table 4.3 regarding the years 1994-96.

Further questions related to the sustainability of fiscal deficits are those concerning demographic shifts, inter-generational equity, and the share of interest payments in total government expenditures. Regarding demographic shifts, Hambor (1992) simulated population trends for several Central and Eastern European countries and derived potential worker/retiree ratios. His analysis suggests that these ratios decline significantly during the next 30 years, although a decade may pass until demographic pressures on pension expenditures may become serious. A declining worker/retiree ratio would, *ceteris paribus*, call for accelerated output growth so as to offset the effect of a larger share of pensioners in the population on disposable incomes. Hence, consideration may be given to the fact that increased present national savings and thus accelerated growth of the capital stock could promote growth.

The discussed risk that fiscal deficits may negatively affect capital formation bears also on inter-generational equity. If this risk would materialize, then, *ceteris paribus*, future generations would receive a lower capital stock compared to the case where today's government expenditures are financed through taxes. However, two cases need to be distinguished, because fiscal deficits can be financed through borrowing or growth in base money (inflation). In the former case, future generations would not only receive a relatively low capital stock but they would also be confronted, *ceteris paribus*, with a stock of public debt that is relatively high. In the case fiscal deficits are financed through growth in base money (inflation), this second burden would not occur. The question would then be whether prevention of a rise in domestic public debt through inflation affects the output growth rate differently than borrowing. In addition, a consideration of inter-generational equity is complicated by the influence of external borrowing on the output growth rate and the difficulty to define welfare of future generations.

Regarding the share of interest payments in total government expenditures, it may be considered that an increase will, *ceteris paribus*, counteract the redistributional function of non-interest government expenditures. Hence, a rising share could make a fiscal deficit unsustainable if it becomes difficult to offset the impact of interest expenditures on the income distribution and if a government becomes unduly constraint in its actions.

Finally, the question has not been discussed whether adjustment should take the form of raising revenues or lowering expenditures. Given the likely deleterious effects for economic growth of tax increases, and given that a decline of the tax revenue to GDP ratio may have to be expected (Tanzi, 1993), it could appear necessary to concentrate on the expenditure side. However, public investment in infrastructure and education are vital for economic growth. Reductions of unemployment benefits and pensions appear to be central in the discussion of fiscal adjustment. They have been analysed by Perraudin (1993): his analysis consists of simulations on the basis of a model of a dynamically optimizing household which includes constraints upon household choices (lifetime wealth, liquidity and employment) to study the likely effects cuts in the welfare system might have on welfare, the fiscal balance, labour supply and savings. The simulations are performed using the data of Poland so that they may not be applicable to other Eastern European countries. However, given that in most Eastern European countries relatively large portions of the populations are pensioners, particularly the results concerning pension benefits appear to be of general importance: an increase of the average period for the derivation of the wage base from which pension entitlements are calculated, raises the effective tax rate on wages.[17] For this case and under the reasonable assumption that (particularly young) consumers face liquidity constraints, a substantial rise of tax revenues and, *ceteris paribus*, national savings is forecast. In addition, tax distortions are likely to be reduced, because the reduction of effective marginal wage tax rates will be distributed over a larger number of periods. Three further results that appear to be of importance for all Eastern European countries are: first, given that a relatively generous welfare system may lower the incentives to save, increased availability of consumer credit (lower borrowing constraints) in the wake of financial liberalization would be expected to negatively affect private savings, unless there are other influences that offset this effect as, for instance, unemployment. Second, cuts in unemployment appear problematic, because they are likely to induce higher earlier retirement. This comes in addition to the danger of increasing poverty. Third, if early retirement would be penalized, the simulations suggest an increase of both tax revenues and national savings. In sum, the simulations suggest that if further reductions in welfare expenditures are intended, then it may be preferable to consider a combination of lower early retirement benefits and a reduction of the base from which pension entitlements are calculated.

To summarize, the relevant question for Eastern European countries regarding sustainability of fiscal deficits appears to be that of optimality which includes, in particular, consideration of the level of national savings, inter-generational equity, and the share of interest expenditures in total government expenditures. Under the condition of a capital stock which is below its optimal level, it appears likely that welfare (proxied by the rate of real output growth) could be raised if present domestic borrowing requirements would be contained so as to provide for a net domestic public debt to GDP ratio which would not increase under the condition of very moderate inflation. Net external borrowing could be regarded as beneficial for economic growth if the domestic return on the resources (adjusted for exchange rate changes) is above the foreign interest rate. However, if there is significant uncertainty regarding this return, it could be preferable not only to stabilize the net domestic public debt to GDP ratio but also the external ratio, particularly if the level of the latter is relatively high: otherwise inflationary expectations could be promoted, because market participants may anticipate that the government pursues restrictive demand policies –

so as to generate external current account surpluses – which, in turn, could result in lower tax revenues and therefore higher inflation.

Notes

1   Stabilization is delayed due to a 'war of attrition' between different socio-economic groups with conflicting distributional objectives. The more uneven is the expected allocation of the costs of stabilization when it occurs, the later is the expected date of stabilization.

2   Spaventa, 1987, p. 375, cites two historical cases: when the overhang of a high debt stock became a primary cause of financial instability and hyperinflation in France in the 1920s, the country's debt to GDP ratio was considerably lower compared to the debt to GDP ratio that prevailed in the United Kingdom for many decades in the 18th century. On the difficulty to determine how large public debts can grow, see Alesina, 1988.

3   The sharp fall in Bulgaria's net external debt ratio during 1992 relates to relatively high inflation concomitant with relatively minor currency depreciation. It appears that during 1992 under-valuation of Bulgaria's currency has been gradually eliminated so that the debt ratio end of 1992 may be more adequate than the end-1991 ratio. A substantial build-up of foreign exchange reserves during 1992 contributed to the decline in Hungary's net external debt ratio.

4   In Poland, the 5 per cent estimate corresponds to somewhat less than one third of outstanding credit to enterprises; on the basis of the data concerning the former Czech and Slovak Federal Republic, the 5 per cent estimate equals about 8 per cent of credit to enterprises.

5   The calculated fiscal adjustment required to restore a government's solvency will not differ under the two approaches, provided government assets are defined narrowly as those that are most likely to be used to service public debt. Both concepts calculate a share of GDP by which the primary balance would have to be adjusted so as to meet the imposed solvency condition.

6   The growth forecasts shown in Table 4.3 are IMF staff estimates. Significantly higher average growth rates for Hungary and Poland during a five year medium-term are forecast by Borensztein and Montiel, 1992. One factor that may provide for relatively high near-term growth are the presently relatively low capital/labour ratios as a consequence of the shocks during transition. However, the measured adjustment of production structures has been relatively minor in all countries during 1991-1992. In addition, political stability has to be taken into account. Therefore, the forecasts shown in Table 4.3 are somewhat less optimistic.

7   Such revenue raising is common in many developing countries. Market

participants pay directly for government services. The major disadvantages of this system are regressivity and relatively high collection costs. However, government revenues in Eastern Europe may continue to be subject to pressure owing to the declining profitability of public enterprises while a further decrease of the share of expenditures in GDP could be difficult to achieve due to financing of unemployment compensation and potential costs associated with privatization of large scale public enterprises. In addition, Eastern European countries experience tax avoidance on a significant scale. Certain tax rates were raised and temporary import surcharges levied. There is a risk that these measures are less efficient than the proposed fees due to the disincentive effects if tax rates, particularly on income, reach relatively high levels and due to avoidance. Tariffs endanger competition, prevent full integration into world markets, and cause additional costs if abolished in future.

8   Table 4.3 shows that the share of Hungary's monetary base in GDP is substantially larger than that in the other countries and hence Hungary could expect relatively large revenues from seignorage. This difference may largely be attributable to the inflation differentials during transition. However, if reserves held by banks at the central bank are interest bearing, seignorage would have to be adjusted by this amount. Taking this qualification into account and provided inflation is contained, expected relatively high growth could make seignorage in Eastern Europe a more important revenue source than in industrial countries, where it yielded about 0.2 per cent of GDP, on average, in the 1980s.

9   The gaps differ slightly from zero, because the critical interest rates are rounded.

10   With the exception of the Czech and Slovak Republics and Hungary, a large part of external debt in Eastern European countries is concessional. In order to calculate the expected debt to GDP ratios at end-1993, a real interest rate of -1 per cent to be paid on external debt was applied with regard to Bulgaria (whose implicit interest payments on external debt stood at about 2 per cent in 1992), a 2 per cent rate with respect to Hungary and a zero per cent rate with regard to Poland and Romania. These interest rates are based on estimates of the degree to which external debt is concessional. The expected real interest rates on domestic public debt shown in Table 4.3 were derived by deflating projected interest payments with the forecast end period (1993) inflation rate.

11   Regarding industrial countries, the empirical evidence suggests that the long run rate of return on capital and thus the long run real interest rate, amounts to about 7-10 per cent (Boskin, 1978). The real return on private capital in Eastern Europe could, for some time to come, conceivably be somewhat higher than the average return in industrial countries if unemployment may be expected to exert some downward pressure on wages and

151

if the tax systems will not be modified. Hence, the assumption of a real interest rate of 5 per cent could appear to be moderate, particularly regarding those countries who service most of their external debt at market rates and thus pay the default risk premium.

12 For instance, the medium-term gap of 2.3 per cent of GDP shown for Bulgaria means that in order to stabilize the end-1992 estimated debt to GDP ratio during the forecast horizon up to 1996, the annual primary surplus would need to be raised by 2.3 percentage points.

13 Table 4.3 illustrates how the required adjustment is influenced through different parameter constellations (initial debt to GDP ratios, primary balances, real interest rates, growth rates, and seignorage).

14 Regarding the asset side, privatization of public enterprises, particularly large ones, could be associated with a net burden for governments, rather than net income, owing to transaction costs and a potential negative net worth of the enterprises in the aggregate. This means that uncertainty of market participants with regard to the primary balances they expect and discount in their assessment of the government's solvency, is pronounced during transition and hence governments could lower the risk premium they pay by providing assurance to markets of future primary balances.

15 The discount rate does not include a risk premium, because the presence of this premium reflects an expectation of insolvency.

16 A permanent increase in government spending will have to be met by a at least an equally large permanent increase in taxes. See the discussion in Appendix III.

17 In Poland, the pension base is the average of labour earnings in the best three of the last 12 years. The Polish authorities intend, however, to increase the averaging period.

5 Concluding remarks

If output in Eastern European countries grows by up to about 2.5 per cent per year, it may not be reasonable to expect unemployment to fall. To reduce it from a level of say 15 per cent to 5 per cent within 5 years, taking a conservative view (an Okun coefficient of 2), could require real output growth per annum of about 6.5 per cent. The recovery of 1932-37 in the United Kingdom and the United States, which was associated with a fall of unemployment by 8.5 percentage points and 14 points, respectively, showed, that rapid improvement is, in principle, feasible, after unemployment has reached a high peak. Capital formation appears to be the condition sine qua non in achieving this growth objective: a rising capital-labour ratio can be expected to raise productivity through several channels, one of which is that of human capital. The latter could also be expected to improve if non-egalitarian income taxation would be maintained. Theoretically, an additional means to raise productivity growth is profit sharing. If the latter is associated with promotion of capital ownership by labour, this could also mitigate distributional conflict and thus prevent wage inflation. However, sharing may require tax incentives so as to prevent two potential adverse effects: reduced profit shares (which would, *ceteris paribus*, tend to reduce productivity growth) and an intensified insider-outsider problem. Since tax incentives pose a new and certain burden for the fiscal balance, whereas the beneficial impact on output growth is uncertain, promotion of profit sharing may not be advisable during transition.

An industrial relations system based on participation, which Eastern European country's espoused by law, poses the question as to the mobility of capital if owners do not have full control, but it bears the potential of promoting productivity. Means to facilitate their voluntary adoption could be seen primarily in measures affecting capital markets: a more even distribution of information through information requirements, establishment of credit rating agencies, promotion of access of small and medium sized firms to capital markets and, in general, long time horizons.

To prevent wage inflation and thus that wage behaviour becomes dependent on the change in employment or unemployment, it appears important that the wage bargaining systems remain centralized and that both parties are well coordinated among themselves. Promotion of the organization of employers' federations, establishment of a parity commission or mediator and promotion of ownership of capital by labour appear to be important means which could facilitate an alignment of wage growth with productivity growth.

Since the constraint on employment growth is productive capital, improving efficiency of the financial system will raise employment, because it implies an increase in capital formation for a given volume of savings. To achieve this, moral hazard would have to be prevented from materializing. Adoption of the BIS rules may not suffice. A preferable definition of own capital could appear to be 'core' capital as defined by the Bank for International Settlements. Setting a relatively high own capital-asset ratio while granting financial intermediaries some flexibility in risk management may achieve both prevention of moral hazard and fulfilment of the risk-taking function of intermediaries. Maintaining the relatively low barriers to entry into financial systems, reducing the latter's implicit taxation (e.g., non-interest bearing reserve requirements, compulsory investment in certain types of securities), privatizing intermediaries following their recapitalization, and encouraging nation-wide operation not limited to certain sectors of the economy could be expected to promote competition (while making the costs of the public sector more transparent). Completion of the array of financial markets may appear less important than concentrating on improving the allocational and operational efficiency of existing ones, although the development of primary securities markets, particularly for equity, would be important.

Given that capital stocks in Eastern Europe appear to be smaller than optimal, domestic financing of fiscal deficits could inhibit growth, because it entails the danger of lowering national savings. Financial liberalization and thus lower constraints on consumer borrowing may pose a further risk for national savings. *ceteris paribus*, external financing of fiscal deficits may be justifiable if there is certainty that the return on the borrowed funds is larger than the foreign interest rate. However, if a reduction of the burden of external debt would be intended so as to increase the share of export revenues that would be available particularly for imports of capital goods, then, in the absence of foreign grants or debt relief, improved competitiveness would be required. Under a fixed exchange rate system, this would necessitate less inflation than that prevailing in competitor countries. If the exchange rate is flexible, depreciations bear the danger of feeding into expectations of inflation and wage formation. Thus in both cases, the preferable way to maintain competitiveness in the long run may appear to be moderate inflation. This could require relative independence of the central bank and strictly defined lending limits for borrowing by the government from the central bank. Under restrictive assumptions, including that of no inflation during 1994-96, the calculated scenarios suggest that stabilization of the estimated total net public debt to GDP ratios is feasible, while paying a positive real interest rate on total net public debt.

Appendix I

Note on the adoption of universal banking systems in Eastern Europe

A comprehensive comparative empirical analysis that concentrates on both the costs and stability of financial intermediation in systems where, on the one hand, the securities business is separated from commercial banking, and, on the other, intermediaries carry out both businesses, appears not to be available. However, developments of financial intermediation in both types of system have been markedly different since the oil price shocks in the 1970s. Countries with universal banking systems experienced substantially less financial innovation of such type whose purpose, in the assessment of some authors, has been to produce accounting profits without contributing to market completeness or enhanced operational efficiency.[1] In addition, the separation of banking from securities business has sparked financial innovations apt to circumvent this regulation. In Japan, the financial system is de facto evolving towards a universal banking system. While it is not controversial that financial system regulation should guard against the potential conflicts of interest, (e.g. conflict between commercial and securities business), and which should be considered in Eastern European banking regulation (perhaps through the so-called 'Chinese walls'), the question arises as to the costs of maintaining rigorous legal separation which is undermined, for instance, by financial innovation. Perhaps more importantly, the costs of financial intermediation (borne by consumers) may be higher in a system of separation, because economies of scale and scope could be prevented from being exploited, which could be particularly eminent in the case of the United States where interstate banking has only gradually been permitted.[2] [3] Although this regulation (McFadden Act) was initially introduced to promote stability of the financial system (through reduced competition), during the past two decades, when international competition intensified, these banks were, *ceteris paribus*, put at a disadvantage to their foreign competitors.[4] Moreover, so-

156

called 'hostile take-overs,' often financed through issuance of high risk securities, have been nearly absent in Germany and Japan. Although it is argued that such activity may improve resource allocation, its existence may induce management behaviour detrimental to stability and growth such as concentration on the short run and increased leverage. The absence of these activities in Germany and Japan could suggest that they are related to the type of financial system. Finally, financial innovation, through its impact on monetary aggregates, impaired monetary targeting and thus may have influenced inflationary expectations. These considerations may corroborate Eastern Europe's decision in favour of universal banking systems but would suggest that in order to fully exploit economies of scale and scope, the relatively large number of small banks should be consolidated. In a competitive process this would result automatically and it could appear preferential to maintain relatively low barriers of entry into the banking market.[5] Since one major factor explaining limited competition in Eastern Europe's banking market appears to be the lack of branch networks, consideration may be given to review the process of granting licenses for the establishment of branches.

Notes

1 See, in particular, van Horne, 1985. Stiglitz and Weiss, 1989 showed that some financial innovations, such as faster recording of transactions, may be welfare reducing. These assessments underline ambiguities concerning often hailed improvements in secondary markets.

2 The following figures provide a rough comparison of the costs of financial intermediation in a system of 'separation' versus a system of universal banks: in the United States, finance and insurance account for 5 per cent of total employment while generating about 6 per cent of GNP (U.S. Department of Commerce, 1992). In Germany, financial intermediation accounts for about 3.6 per cent of total employment and 5 per cent of GNP (Statistisches Bundesamt, 1992). The figures represent only value added by labour and capital directly employed.

3 Recent empirical analyses of economies of scale and scope relate almost exclusively to banks in the United States and Canada. Clark (1988) provides an overview concerning studies that examined these economies in banks in the United States, Canada, and Israel, and which were carried out in the mid-1980s, covering the period 1975-1983. Commonly, a trans-log cost function is estimated and universal existence of economies of scale is confirmed up to an output (measured in terms of deposits) of about US\$ 100 million. Universal existence of economies of scope is not confirmed although there appear to exist product specific economies of scope. Regarding analysis of large banks, Shaffer (1988) used alternative func-

tional forms to test for robustness of results. For the largest 100 commercial banks in the United States he finds small but significant economies of scale up to an output (consolidated assets) of about US\$ 60 billion. Hence, results regarding banks in the United States are somewhat inconsistent. In addition, they may not be applicable to other countries. A cautious approach regarding banking systems in Eastern Europe could be to assume existence of very limited economies of scale and scope.

4   It should be noted that the 'savings and loan associations" crisis in the United States during the latter half of the 1980s may not be evaluated as a deficiency of the U.S. financial system. The crisis was triggered by deregulation (permitting savings and loan associations to invest in assets associated with relatively high risk and through liberalized interest rates) resulting in materialization of both moral hazard and term-structure risk.

5   The paid-in capital requirement within the EC, currently set at ECU 5 million, could serve as a benchmark.

Appendix II

The money supply process in Eastern European countries

I. Introduction

The following multiplier model of supply of and demand for broad money may serve as an illustration of the money supply process in Eastern European countries. Specifically, a 'credit crunch' as a result of macroeconomic instability caused by excessive base money growth is conceivable even in a competitive banking market. Banks curtail lending if the expected return on loans, adjusted for losses covered by a third party, is below its opportunity costs such as the return on securities issued by the government. But such behaviour, which is (constraint) efficient because it protects the economy from output losses and is merely the mirror image of inconsistent policies, occurs only if moral hazard is contained. Lending in Eastern European countries has generally been tight, independent of the evolution of measures of real interest rates.[1] It has been suggested that this occurred owing to uncompetitive credit markets, credit ceilings, and government guidance aiming at promoting prudent bank behaviour. In addition, text Table 6 showed that banks' loanable funds decreased (except in Hungary). This may be part of the explanation, but it is also possible for the moral hazard problem on the part of both banks and public nonfinancial enterprises not to have been contained. The model shows that under this circumstance, a rise in lending would be expected, provided the expected real interest rate is positive, which requires then reconciliation with actual developments. Rising inter enterprise arrears may provide this reconciliation. It will become evident how important prudential regulation of banks is (particularly under macroeconomic instability), or preferably, the setting of incentives for banks to contain risk, for instance, through high required equity. The aim should be not to permit the latent moral hazard problem (due to an expected

159

bail-out by the government) to influence bank behaviour.

Banking markets in Eastern Europe may not be particularly competitive, (reinforcing the argument that banks keep spreads high through restrained lending), but participation of foreign banks could be expected for borrowers, at least those with highest credit rating, to be offered an alternative, triggering competition in this market segment. Presence of a large number of small banks in each of the six Eastern European countries could, if policies permit through encouragement of branching, result in a process where efficient banks take over inefficient ones and eventually operate nation-wide or even internationally. However, although it is the oligopoly under which competition can be most fierce, most credit markets in industrial countries under universal banking, which appear to be oligopolistic markets, are nevertheless characterized by a limited degree of competition and therefore uncompetitiveness has to be taken seriously.

II. The model [2]

It is assumed that there are only two assets in which banks can invest: a risk-free asset (money market instruments issued by the government (B_{MM})), and loans to enterprises and private households (K). Banks need to hold reserves (R) against deposits of which there are two types: demand deposits (non-interest bearing (D)) and time deposits (T), the return on the latter (i_T) being assumed to increase with a rise in the lending interest rate (i_L). Markets are assumed to be competitive so that interest rates are given and banks are profit maximizers optimizing their portfolio. The only item on their liabilities side which they can influence is refinancing at the central bank (rediscounting, lombard borrowing, repurchase agreements).

The balance sheet restrictions for the banking system outside the central bank and the consolidated banking system (including the central bank), form the basic identities, supplemented by behavioural equations for the allocation of deposits (on the part of enterprises and private households), the time and savings deposit interest rate, the supply of loans, and the demand for broad money. The consolidated balance sheet of the banking system is given by:

(1) $B' + K = C + D + T$

where B' denotes adjusted base money (sum of foreign exchange reserves, net credit to the public sector, money market instruments (short term government papers) held by banks minus net worth of the central bank),[3] K denotes loans, C denotes domestic currency held outside the banking system, D are demand deposits and T are time and savings deposits. The balance sheet restriction for the banking system, excluding the central bank, reads:

(2) $R + B_{MM} + K = D + T + F$

where R denotes reserve requirements, B_{MM} are money market instruments (short term government bonds), and F is refinancing of banks at the central bank.[4] Reserve requirements are a fraction of demand, and time deposits and there are no excess reserves:

$$(3) \quad R = \alpha (D + T) \ , \qquad \alpha > 0$$

where α is the ratio of required reserves (assumed to be unified). Money market instruments (B_{MM}) are assumed to be traded only in the official money market so that only banks' investment in loans but not securities increases the money supply. Their return is given by i_{MM}, which, to simplify, is set by the central bank.[5] The central bank also determines the discount rate (z), (applied to all refinancing facilities), and the amount of refinancing offered (Q). A proportional relation between banks' investment in money market instruments and deposits (adjusted for required reserves) is assumed, and, *ceteris paribus*, holding of these securities will be a negative function of both the lending rate (i_L) and the discount rate (z) and a positive function of their return (i_{MM}) and of refinancing facilities (Q). Thus, banks' portfolio selection yields the following demand function for these instruments:

$$(4) \quad B_{MM} = \beta \ (\overset{-}{i_L}, \ \overset{+}{i_{MM}} \ , \ \overset{-}{z} \ , \overset{+}{Q}) \ [(D + T) \ (1 - r)] \ , \beta > 0$$

Signs above arguments indicate the sign of the first partial derivative of β with respect to the respective argument.

Total deposits held by enterprises and private households are allocated among time deposits, on the one hand, and demand deposits, on the other, dependent on the coefficient t, which, in turn, is a positive function of the return on time i_T. The latter return depends positively on i_L:

$$(5) \quad T = t (\overset{+}{i_T}) D \ ,$$

$$(5a) \quad i_T = \overset{+}{i_L}$$

Banks' decision to supply credit will be, *ceteris paribus*, a negative function of the rediscount rate (z), and a positive function of refinancing facilities (Q). The supply may be assumed to increase proportionally with available deposits (adjusted for required reserves). The influence of the lending rate on bank behaviour depends on prudential regulation of banks (denoted X, consisting of regulation of own capital, risk taking and loan loss provisioning). Provided there exists no moral hazard problem, for instance due to adequate regulation of banks, and given that loans are associated with risk, their expected rate of return will rise with the lending rate i_L only up to a critical rate denoted i_L^* (Stiglitz and Weiss, 1981). A lending rate above this level would entail a decrease of the

161

expected return for three reasons: since information is asymmetric between the bank and borrowers, the bank assumes that creditworthy borrowers are less inclined to borrow at this high interest rate level (adverse selection effect). Second, the bank anticipates that the remaining less creditworthy borrowers tend to choose investment projects associated with a higher risk so as to raise expected profits (adverse incentive effect). Third, if the rise in the (expected real) lending interest rate is due to inflation concomitant with macroeconomic instability, the variance in the return from borrowers' investment projects is likely to increase and positive correlation among these variances arises (positive covariances) (McKinnon, 1988). In other words, the systemic or undiversifiable risk in the economy increases. Thus, supply of credit becomes a negative function of the lending rate when the bank expects the effect of macroeconomic instability on the repayment probability to exceed the impact on the real lending rate and hence returns on loans to decline. In addition, risk-sharing in the form of an implicit contract (Fried and Howitt, 1980) between the bank and borrower, defined as a lending rate that is stable relative to the opportunity costs of loanable funds, may break down with a rise in interest rates due to macroeconomic instability.[6] The reason is that increasing uncertainty regarding the evolution of opportunity costs will shorten the planning horizon of the bank. The economic costs of entering into long-term contracts become prohibitive. Hence, constraint efficient and thus welfare increasing credit rationing (backward bending credit supply curve), characterized by implicit contracts, may be assumed to occur only if moral hazard does not materialize, due to prudential regulation. Moral hazard is always present and reinforced if deposits are insured. The question is how it is contained so as to prevent adverse externalities. A bank maximizes expected profits and hence takes losses into account that are covered by the government and/or deposit insurance.[7] If there is significant sharing in losses, the bank may not ration credit but rationally increase lending with a rise of the lending rate and thus take higher risk, because its expected profits continue to rise. The credit supply function may thus be written:

(6) $\quad K^S = \gamma(i_L, i_{MM}, z, Q, X)[(D+T)(1-r)]$

with x = 1, *if prudential regulation is effective, otherwise* x = 0

$$\gamma > 0; \quad \frac{\delta\gamma}{\delta i_L} > 0 \;\; \textit{if} \;\; X = 0, \;\; \frac{\delta\gamma}{\delta i_L} > 0 \;\; \textit{if} \;\; X = 1 \wedge i_L < i_L^*,$$

$$\frac{\delta\gamma}{\delta i_L} < 0, \;\; \textit{if} \;\; X = 1 \wedge i_L > i_L^*; \quad \frac{\delta\gamma}{\delta i_{MM}} < 0; \;\; \frac{\delta\gamma}{\delta z} < 0; \;\; \frac{\delta\gamma}{\delta Q} > 0$$

Domestic currency (C) is held as a fixed proportion of demand deposits:

(7) $C = kD$

Broad money is defined as:

(8) $M = C + D + T$

Setting equilibrium conditions for the loan market and market for broad money would close the model, if it were not rational for banks to ration credit. Because of (constraint) efficient credit rationing, both markets exhibit excess demand. Substituting equations (5), (6), and (7) into (1), and solving for demand deposits yields:

(9) $$D = \frac{1}{1 + k + t - \gamma(1+t)(1-r)} \dot{B}$$

Setting M equal to broad money supply (M^S) (equation (8)), and after some algebraic manipulation, one obtains the money supply multiplier:

(10) $$M^S = \frac{1 + k + t}{(1+t)[1 - \gamma(1-r)] + k} \dot{B}$$

With prudent behaviour of banks, γ decreases, *ceteris paribus*, as i_L rises above the critical lending rate i_L^*, and hence, the multiplier decreases resulting in a falling money supply.[8] With non-prudent behaviour, γ is likely to increase and so would the money supply with credit allocated to high risk projects, implying a relatively high probability for loans not to perform and thus relatively lower steady state growth.

Turning to the demand for broad money, real money demand (L^r) is assumed to be a function of i_L, i_T, real income (Y^r) and expected inflation (π^*). Increases in the latter affect real money demand negatively, not only through economizing on holdings but also through currency substitution which is facilitated by current account convertibility.[9] Nominal money demand (L) is assumed to be homogenous of degree one in the price level. Using equations (5), (7) and (8), the demand for broad money becomes:

(11) $$L = \frac{1 + k + t}{1 + k} L^r (\overset{-}{i_L}, \overset{-}{i_T}, \overset{+}{Y^r}, \overset{-}{\pi^*}) p$$

where L^r is the demand for real narrow money and L denotes the nominal demand for broad money.

III. Lending behaviour of banks

Fig. AII.1 demonstrates the difference between a system in which credit rationing occurs ($X = 1$) and one in which moral hazard materializes ($X = 0$). (The latter being characterized by a continuously upward sloping credit supply curve). With adequate equity requirements and effective prudential supervision, the supply curve bends backward. The optimal lending interest rate i_L^* (equal to the critical rate where the expected return to the bank reaches its maximum) determines the supply of credit. Credit in the amount AC is rationed out. Money demand exceeds money supply in the amount BD. The money supply will be M^* of which K^{S*} is supply of loans with the remainder being adjusted base money (B').

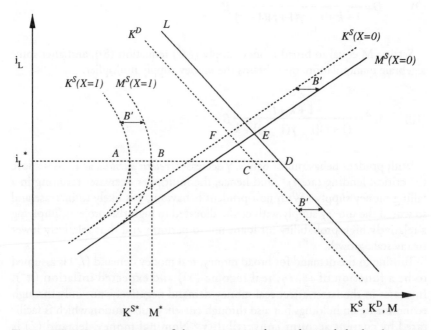

Figure AII.1 Determination of the money supply, credit, and the lending rate of interest

For at least two reasons the model lends itself well in analysing the money supply process in Eastern European countries: capital markets are bank-based so that shifts into and out of securities or other non-monetary assets on the part of non-banks may remain negligible, provided credible disinflationary policies are

164

pursued. (In the model, portfolio choice by non-banks is crudely incorporated through the parameters k and t). Second, interest rates are, in principle, liberalized, with subsidization of loans apparently intended to be limited to housing, so that the main transmissionary mechanism of monetary policy would be credit availability (under credit rationing) or interest rates (if there is no credit rationing). The exchange rate could, however, be an important additional transmissionary channel in countries with a managed exchange rate regime (Bulgaria, Poland, Romania), particularly when indexation of wages to the consumer price level is present. Credit availability and interest rates are controlled through adjusted base money and the central bank's influence on the multiplier through affecting bank lending behaviour (γ).

Four theoretical cases both under competitive markets and then under uncompetitive markets shall be considered in an attempt to explain bank lending behaviour: (i) effective regulation concomitant with money supply growth expected by market participants to correspond to real output growth (presence of this expectation being defined as 'stability' and, if absent, defined as 'instability'); (ii) ineffective regulation with stability; (iii) effective regulation with instability; (iv) ineffective regulation with instability.

(i) the above described 'equilibrium with rationing' characterized by point B in Fig. AII.1 prevails. Money demand may be assumed to be both relatively stable and interest elastic (with the yield curve likely to slope upwards so that savings and hence growth are promoted). Banks ration credit but there is no reason for a credit crunch to occur unless banks evaluate borrowers creditworthiness to be substandard and thus invest in government securities.

(ii) banks are likely to take excessive risk and satisfy credit demand. The credit and money markets are in equilibrium at points F and E, respectively. The economy could suffer output losses owing to nonperforming loans.

(iii): B' increases above real output growth. The short run model response would be that K^S ($X=1$) and M^S ($X=1$) shift rightwards, whereas K^D would shift leftwards resulting in lower interest rates. However, if inflation is high, nominal money demand increases although real money demand declines, causing higher interest rates and the three above described adverse effects. Hence, the K^S curve may shift relatively little to the right although M^S expands strongly. Most of the nominal money demand is satisfied through base money with revenues from the inflation tax declining, *ceteris paribus*, if real money demand falls. Banks invest mainly in government papers. Real credit declines and despite a possibly steeply and positively sloped yield curve, long term credit may be rationed out.

(iv) banks do not ration credit but take excessive risk and the likelihood for loans to become nonperforming is larger than in case (ii), owing to the three adverse effects.

Under uncompetitive markets, the credit supply curves shift upward with the spread between lending and deposit rates being increased (resulting, *ceteris paribus*, in lower savings and investment). Other modifications appear unlikely except in case (iii) (effective regulation and instability with the credit supply curve being K^S $(X = 1)$). Here, a credit crunch occurs and banks may invest mainly in loans to the government and, if there is collusion among banks, it could appear likely that they would attempt to extract rent from the market for loans and the market for government securities. The government has a monopoly position but it may be in a weaker position than banks if it recognizes that it should finance fiscal deficits through domestic and/or external borrowing and not through growth of the monetary base in order to prevent a further rise in inflation and thus also a likely further adverse impact on real growth and the tax base of inflation. Hence, in addition to the credit crunch, a redistribution of income could occur if banks incur a rent on cost of tax payers.

Which case may characterize the situation in Eastern Europe? The evolution of inflation diverges: in the Czech and Slovak Republics, and Hungary it appears to be contained with inflationary expectations possibly at a rather moderate level so that the case of 'stability' could be a rough approximation (see also text Table 3.4). In Bulgaria and Romania, owing to the continuing build-up of inter-enterprise arrears and apparently relatively less stringent so-called 'hard-budget constraints' for public enterprises, expectations could be such that 'instability' prevails, resulting in the two adverse behavioural effects and positive covariance of returns on investment projects. The developments in Poland may appear more difficult to assess. The question is then which implicit degree of prudential regulation of banks prevails (e.g. reputation of a bank, 'toughness' of a government so that private banks do not expect a 'bail-out' through the government in case of losses), given that explicit regulation appears inadequate (text Table 4). Implicit regulation appears to be weak for four reasons: first, banks in Eastern Europe are being privatized only since recently with the largest banks still government owned so that these banks may not be permitted to fail; second, governments extended guarantees for interest capitalization, possibly creating an expectation of further bail-out; third, public enterprises in arrears could coerce banks into extending more credit, because bankruptcy laws were introduced only recently (Bulgaria and Romania) or are not effective due to the economic costs for the bank if it was to force the borrower into bankruptcy; fourth, if time horizons are relatively short, reputation may not be a significant factor. Hence, it would appear reasonable to assume moral hazard to materialize. As already noted, actual developments could suggest that this assessment does not hold: credit ceilings were not fully used where measures of real lending interest rates were positive and high (e.g., Bulgaria), and lending has generally been relatively tight. Credit rationing may have occurred with banks preferring to lend to the government. However, generally rising inter-enterprise arrears provide an explanation, particularly with regard to countries characterized by 'instability:' public enterprises' credit demand proved not interest inelastic so that borrowing from banks was substituted for by less expensive borrowing from enterprises (even though interest payment on the latter has generally become mandatory). Where ex-post real lending and deposit rates have been negative (e.g., Romania), an additional factor may contribute to a decline in credit: demand would, *ceteris paribus*, be promoted, but banks lending base would, *ceteris paribus*, decline, resulting in the supply curve to shift leftwards. In sum, the main reason why lending has been relatively tight during transition may be seen in a leftward shift of credit demand. Inter-enterprise borrowing was substituted for borrowing from banks.

IV. Outlook
Finally, the model may be used to provide an outlook regarding control of the money supply. Given underdeveloped securities markets and restricted capital flows, control of the monetary base may not be significantly impaired through shifts in portfolios of domestic assets and capital movements. If the central bank would have control over the monetary base, the question would then become mainly whether M in Eastern Europe should be defined such as to include foreign currency deposits? Presently, the latter are included in definitions of broad money applied in Eastern Europe. The model abstracted from this fact. Including foreign currency deposits (FC) in the definition of money, equation (8) becomes:

(8a) $M' = C + D + T + FC$

Foreign currency deposits may be assumed to be a positive function of expected inflation; domestic demand deposits, required to finance transactions, could be a scalar variable.

Money supply then becomes:

(12) $FC = f(\overset{+}{\pi^*})D$

(10a) $M^S = \dfrac{1+k+t+f}{(1+t+f)-[1-\gamma(1-r)]+k} B'$

and money demand may be written:

(11a) $L' = \dfrac{1+k+t+f}{1+k} L^{r'} (\overset{-}{i_L}, \overset{-}{i_T}, \overset{+}{Y^r}, \overset{-}{\pi^*}) p$

where $L^{r'}$ now comprises the demand for domestic money balances and foreign currency. A rise in π^* will cause a substitution of foreign currency deposits for domestic time and savings deposits, because the latter loose their property as a store of wealth. At the same time desired real money balances are affected. The preceding analysis assumes that reserve requirements on foreign currency deposits do not differ from the assumed identical requirements on domestic demand and time deposits (r). In Eastern European countries, regulations concerning reserve requirements vary significantly so that the multipliers differ. For instance, in Poland, relatively high requirements are levied on demand, time, and savings deposits whereas foreign currency deposits are presently not 'taxed.' Hence, creation of foreign currency deposits by banks is, *ceteris paribus*, facilitated. This may have an impact on the domestic inflation rate. It could thus appear preferable to impose reserve requirements on foreign currency deposits. Given that reserve requirements may retain importance for years to come as a form of substitute for insufficient bank equity, insufficient loan loss provisions, and possibly insufficient risk management, their lowering may not be advisable. Relatively high reserve requirements have the additional advantage of making the multiplier smaller, *ceteris paribus*, thus improving control of the money supply. The associated implicit taxation of banks could be eliminated if reserve requirements would bear interest.

The central factor influencing the money supply process may be seen, however, in inflationary expectations. Within the above framework the positive effect of contained inflationary expectations becomes apparent: changes in k, t, and f are likely to decline and stabilize if economic agents expect the government to pursue restrictive and time consistent policies. Domestic currency deposits would then be likely to crowd out foreign currency holdings, and desired real money balances may rise. As soon as it may become feasible to forecast growth of potential real output with a reasonable degree of accuracy, money demand could then be forecast as well. If the central bank would have control over the monetary base, achievement of an inflation target by means of monetary targeting could then become an alternative to an exchange rate target.

Notes

1   Although relatively volatile, for the most part during the first 24 months of transition, ex-post measures of real lending interest rates have been positive in Bulgaria, Hungary, and Poland, while negative in the Czech and Slovak Republics, and Romania. With the decline in inflation after the initial adjustment phase, ex-post measures of real lending rates, but not real deposit rates, became positive in the Czech and Slovak Republics.

2   The multiplier approach has its roots in the work mainly by Brunner and Meltzer (see, for instance, Brunner and Meltzer, 1968). The model utilized here is a modified version of those in Jarchow, 1987, pp. 156-174, and Siebke, 1972.

3   This concept of the monetary base is helpful, because it provides a measure

of base money that is solely controlled by the central bank and thus independent of banks' behaviour. It can be written $B' = B - (F - B_{MM})$, where B is the conventional monetary base (reserves plus currency held by banks and enterprises), F is refinancing provided by the central bank, and B_{MM} denotes money market instruments usable for refinancing.

4   To stress the importance of equity is one purpose of this appendix. Nevertheless, it is not included in the balance sheet restriction, because this consideration would not have an influence on bank *behaviour* in the model. In the model the influence of equity is exogenous.

5   In reality, in Eastern Europe, where capital flows are restricted and hence central banks are rather free to determine interest rates, it is a function of the amount of papers issued.

6   The gain of an implicit contract for the bank consists in maintaining long term customer relationships so that information costs decrease.

7   In general, risk-taking is promoted if a government shares equally in gains and losses (which may be assumed to spur growth under macroeconomic stability). However, given the central position of financial intermediaries in economic activity, promotion of risk-taking on the part of these entities does not appear justifiable. The recommendation made in Section 2.4 for insurance companies to be permitted to invest in equity does not contradict this assessment, because provided such investments are long term and diversified, they are likely, *ceteris paribus*, to stabilize an economy and lift in on a higher growth path with earnings of these institutions rising.

8   The positive impact of a rise in the lending interest rate on t (equations (5) and (5a)) does not affect broad money but its composition.

9   Capital outflows cannot be prevented under current account convertibility, because invoices of imports for goods and services may be manipulated. Their official restriction increases transaction costs for them. This does not mean, however, that they should be liberalized. Transaction costs may be sufficiently high to contain them so as to subsidize domestic banks and enterprises during transition (infant industry argument).

Appendix III

Note on the intertemporal government budget constraint

When all variables except the interest rate, the inflation rate, and the growth rate of GNP are expressed as ratios to GNP, the government's one period budget identity can be written as:

$$(1) \quad \dot{b} = g - \tau + (i - p - y)b - \frac{\dot{M}}{Y}$$

where:
$\dot{b}$ = change in the debt to GNP ratio
b = net public debt to GNP ratio
g = ratio of spending of the consolidated government on goods and services (excluding interest expenditures) plus net transfers to GNP
τ = ratio of tax revenues to GNP
i = nominal interest rate
p = inflation rate
y = rate of growth of real GNP
M = stock of high-powered money
$\dot{M}$ = change in high-powered money
Y = nominal GNP

Denoting the primary (non-interest) deficit to GNP ratio with d ($d = g - \tau$) and the real interest rate with r ($r = i - p$) gives:

$$(2) \quad \dot{b} = d + (r - y)b - \frac{\dot{M}}{Y}$$

Equation (2) shows how the ratio of the stock of debt to GNP grows over time. It equals the primary deficit to GNP ratio plus the real interest rate adjusted for real output growth multiplied by the initial period debt ratio less the revenue from seigniorage. If the interest rate on debt exceeds the rate of output growth, the government must run a primary surplus, adjusted for revenues from seignorage, sufficient to offset the effect on the debt ratio of the excess of the interest rate over the growth rate. Otherwise, the debt ratio would increase infinitely. On the other hand, with r < y, the debt ratio will grow at a declining rate and will eventually remain constant even when there is a constant primary deficit and debt is serviced by further borrowing. In this case, the government does not face a solvency constraint. However, theoretical reasoning suggests not to concentrate on this case. When r < y, the debt to GNP ratio could grow to an undetermined high level. This raises the question as to the potential effects for financial stability if real interest rates became positive or, assuming positive output growth, if the economy were hit by an external or domestic exogenous shock that would cause a rise in the interest rate or a decline in the growth rate of output or both.[1] The expectation that such a shock would undermine the stability of the system appears not to be speculative. The government would find itself in a dilemma: it would either have to take action to reduce the primary deficit or to reduce the real debt stock by means of inflation and/or debt repudiation. All of these actions would have detrimental effects on economic activity. A government that is risk averse must therefore be assumed to set up its fiscal plan under the constraint that $r > y$, even when there have been periods during which this condition was not satisfied.[2]

Assuming that growth of the high-powered money stock equals nominal GNP growth:

$$\frac{\dot{M}}{M} = y + p = \lambda$$

equation (1) can be written as:

(1a) $\quad \dot{b} = g - \tau + (r - y)b - \lambda m$

where $m = M/Y$.

When summing a succession of single period budget constraints of the form of equation (1a) over an infinite planning horizon, one obtains the intertemporal budget constraint in terms of present discounted values:

(3) $\quad b_t = \int_t^\infty \tau_s e^{-(r-y)(s-t)} ds - \int_t^\infty g_s e^{-(r-y)(s-t)} ds$

$\qquad + \int_t^\infty \lambda_s m_s e^{-(r-y)(s-t)} ds + \lim_{s \to \infty} b_s e^{-(r-y)(s-t)}$

Imposing government solvency, namely the condition that, in the long run, the growth rate of public debt should be smaller than the interest rate, implies that debt should not be serviced indefinitely by borrowing so that:

171

(4) $\lim_{s \to \infty} b_s e^{-(r-y)(s-t)} = 0$

and the intertemporal budget constraint is expressed by:

(5) $b_t = \int_t^\infty \tau_s e^{-(r-y)(s-t)} ds - \int_t^\infty g_s e^{-(r-y)(s-t)} ds$

$\qquad + \int_t^\infty \lambda_s m_s e^{-(r-y)(s-t)} ds$

Equation (5) shows that the initial debt to GNP ratio must equal the sum of the ratio of expected future primary surpluses to GNP and the ratio of expected future seignorage to GNP. Under solvency, debt is not serviced indefinitely by borrowing, and thus debt must be serviced by primary surpluses and/or seignorage, or, in other words, a permanent increase in government spending must be matched by at least an equally large permanent increase in taxes (seignorage being regarded as a tax), implying that policy makers do not have a choice between a permanently higher level of taxes and a permanently higher level of debt (Feldstein, 1985 p. 244)). However, several considerations cause the intertemporal budget constraint to appear as a rather weak criterion of sustainability of fiscal deficits and debt growth. As shown by McCallum (1984), the growth of debt is not bounded by equation (5) and there exists no finite stationary value for b. All fiscal rules that meet the intertemporal budget constraint are compatible with optimal equilibrium in a model of rational agents with perfect foresight and infinite horizons, even if the rules cause unbounded growth of debt and taxation. Spaventa (1987) provides a survey of fiscal rules that make the debt, and possibly the borrowing requirement, grow forever. Thus, defining sustainability of fiscal policy as the fulfilment of the intertemporal budget constraint assumes that there are no limits to the levels of taxation that society would tolerate. Consequently, it must be assumed that a rising tax burden will not have significant negative effects on the tax base, the incentive to work, and that the distribution of income will not be affected such that destabilizing social reactions are raised. In addition, even when growth of debt is bounded, the limit may be very high and the time profile of debt growth is undetermined.

Notes

1   Equation (2) holds both in nominal and real terms.
2   It may be noted that in steady state, assuming no population growth, the interest rate would equal the growth rate of GNP, because productivity growth would determine both the marginal product of capital and thus the interest rate and also growth.

Appendix IV

Translation of the intertemporal government budget constraint into an operational criterion

1. The budget gap or tax gap approach

On an ex-post basis the government's intertemporal budget constraint (equation 5) will always be met by means of fiscal consolidation, monetary financing and/or even debt repudiation. The issue is, however, whether the constraint is violated by a given fiscal and monetary plan on an ex-ante basis. Will there be a need for readjustment of the plan and, if so, of what magnitude? One way to translate the intertemporal budget constraint into an operational criterion is that suggested by Blanchard (1990). Sustainability of fiscal policy is defined on two major premises, as discussed in the text: first, it does not appear possible to derive an optimal public debt to GNP ratio for a given country and second, debt cannot be serviced indefinitely by issuing new debt. On this basis, a fiscal plan over a given time horizon is defined to be sustainable if a terminal debt to GNP ratio equal to the initial one is achieved. Supposing that the initial debt to GNP ratio and the sequences of g and t (government expenditures and tax revenues as per cent of GNP) are given, what is the constant tax rate, t_n^*, which insures sustainability such that b in n years is the same as b_0? This tax rate is given by:

$$(6) \quad t_n^* = (r - y)\{(1 - \exp{-(r - y)n})^{-1}[\int(g)\exp{-(r - y)s\,ds}] + b_0\}$$

As n approaches infinity, t_n^* approaches t^*. As an approximation, it may be stated that the tax rate t_n^* equals the average value of g over n years, plus the interest rate net of growth times initial debt:

$$(7) \qquad t_n^* = \frac{\sum\limits_{j=0}^{n} g_j}{n} + (r - y)b_0$$

Subtracting t from both sides of equation (7), one obtains the adjustment in the tax ratio required to stabilize the public debt to GNP ratio over the period considered and given the projected path of noninterest expenditures, real growth of GNP (both expressed as ratios to GNP), and the real interest rate:

$$(8) \qquad t_n^* - t = \frac{\sum\limits_{j=0}^{n} g_j}{n} + (r - y)b_0 - t$$

Equation (8) measures the 'tax gap'[1] to achieve sustainability and is used to calculate one forward looking indicator with the value chosen for n being three years so that the forecast extends up to the fiscal year 1996. Despite the obvious difficulties connected with the forecast of tax revenues, expenditures, real interest rate and real growth of GDP up to 1996, the construction of such an indicator may be useful so as to obtain additional information in the evaluation of the consistency of the current fiscal plans. A positive difference between t* and the current tax rate t indicates a need for a tightening of fiscal policy.

In addition to this forward looking indicator, a third and simple one is commonly used that does not rely on forecasts, namely the primary gap as suggested by equation (2). Setting the change in the debt stock in equation (2) equal to zero, the primary budget gap can be written:

$$(9) \qquad s^* - s = (r - y)\, b - s$$

where s = primary surplus $(= -d)$.

The primary gap equals the difference between the primary surplus that stabilizes the outstanding public debt to GNP ratio and the current primary fiscal deficit. Since this indicator does not take into account future official budgetary projections, it may give a misleading signal about the underlying fiscal situation. However, its advantage is that it requires minimal information, namely the present primary balance, the base year public debt to GDP or GNP ratio, and trend real interest rates and output growth.

2. The forward looking balance sheet approach

The government's intertemporal budget constraint can also be written in form of a forward looking balance sheet that comprises the government's assets and liabilities so as to assess the net worth. There is no conceptual difference between this approach and the budget- or tax gap. The approach was suggested by Buiter (1983) and recently discussed in Guidotti and Kumar (1991).

The following equation presents the forward looking government's balance sheet in terms of domestic currency:

(10) $EA^* + R = G + S + B + EB^* + K$

where G, S, and R denote the present values of expected government expenditures, subsidies, and tax and non-tax revenues. A asterisk denotes the stock of foreign exchange reserves, B and B^* denote domestic and external government debt, respectively. E denotes the exchange rate and K provides a measure of a government's net worth. Government assets appear on the LHS of the identity and comprise two parts, the current stock of assets and the present value of anticipated future revenues from tax and non-tax revenues, including seignorage. However, only those assets are considered that are most likely to be used to service public debt. Government liabilities appear on the RHS and comprise also two groups: the current outstanding stock of debt and other current obligations and the present value of future expenditures, including subsidies, transfers, and net lending and equity participation. The government's solvency is defined with regard to K, the government's net worth. Since the balance sheet considers particular assets only, the approach is based upon a particular notion of net worth and solvency, namely that which relates to the ability of the government to service its liabilities. K is the variable used in assessing this ability. If assets exceed liabilities, then the net worth is positive and the government is able to meet its current and future obligations. In this case, it is regarded as being solvent. If the net worth is negative, then the government is not able to meet its contractual debt obligations. Turning to the implications of this approach, equation (10) shows that for a given net worth to be maintained, an increase in public debt must be matched by either an increase in the present value of revenues or current assets and/or a decrease in the present value of expenditures. The changes in revenues and/or expenditures comprise both current and expected fiscal adjustments. Thus, the approach demonstrates the fundamental equivalence of expected government expenditures, domestic and external debt. If a country is expected to run increasing fiscal deficits, this is equivalent to an increase in present government domestic or external debt and may cause a solvency problem. Consider the case of a government whose balance sheet net worth is zero. If markets expect higher future fiscal deficits with foreign assets remaining constant, the only means that prevents the net worth from becoming negative is a reduction in the market value of domestic and/or external debt. Thus, a potential consequence of such an expectation consists in a decrease of secondary market prices of the country's domestic and external debt.[2]

In sum, the forward looking balance sheet approach underscores the importance of expectations in determining whether a government is solvent or not.

Present and expected government expenditures and revenues, public net domestic and net external debt, and the discount rate determine solvency.

Notes

1 The tax gap may also be called budget gap, because what is measured is the adjustment required in per cent of GNP or GDP.

2 However, if markets have the perception that the government's willingness to service its debt differs with regard to domestic debt on the one hand and external debt on the other hand, then the necessary decline in the market value of total debt can be brought about by differing shares of the burden that fall on these two types of debt. For instance, an announcement by a government that it will restrict the servicing of its external debt to a certain percentage of total export receipts would, *ceteris paribus*, give domestic debt seniority over external debt. Guidotti and Kumar (1991) discuss further implications of government insolvency.

176

References

Section 2

Aghevli, Bijan B., Eduardo Borensztein, and Tessa van der Willigen (1992), 'Stabilization and structural reform in the Czech and Slovak Federal Republic: first stage', *Occasional Paper* no. 92, International Monetary Fund, Washington, D.C..

Aoki, Masahiko (1988), Information, *Incentives and Bargaining in the Japanese Economy*, London.

Atkinson, Anthony B., and John Micklewright (1991), 'Unemployment compensation and labor market transitions: a critical review', *Journal of Economic Literature*, vol. 29, December, pp. 1679-1727.

Baily, Martin N. (1981), 'Productivity and the services of capital and labor', *Brookings Papers on Economic Activity*, no. 1, pp. 1-50.

Blanchard, Olivier J., and Lawrence H. Summers (1988), 'Beyond the natural rate hypothesis', *American Economic Review. Papers and Proceedings*, vol. 78, no. 2, May, pp. 182-187.

Blasi, Joseph R., (1990) 'Comment on: Participation, Productivity, and the Firm's Environment', by David Levine and Laura D'Andrea Tyson, in: Blinder, Alan S. (ed.), *Paying for Productivity. A Look at the Evidence*, The Brookings Institution, Washington, D.C., pp. 1-13.

Blinder, Alan S. (1990), Introduction in: Blinder, Alan S. (ed.), *Paying for Productivity. A Look at the Evidence*, The Brookings Institution, Washington, D.C., pp. 1-13.

Calmfors, L. and J. Driffill (1988), 'Centralization of wage bargaining and macroeconomic performance', *Economic Policy*, no. 6, pp. 13-61.

Calvo, Guillermo, and Jacob A. Frenkel (1991), 'Obstacles to transforming centrally-planned economies: the role of capital markets', International Monetary Fund, unpublished Working Paper, July.

____, ____ (1992), 'Transformation of centrally planned economies: credit markets and sustainable growth', in: Winckler, Georg (ed.), *Central and Eastern Europe Roads to Growth*, Papers presented at a seminar held in Baden, Austria April 15-18, 1991. International Monetary Fund, Austrian National Bank, Washington, D.C., pp. 111-137.

Chadha, Bankim (1991), 'Wages, profitability, and growth in a small open economy', *Staff Papers*, International Monetary Fund, vol. 38, no.1, March, pp. 59-82.

Clark, John Bates (1899), *The Distribution of Wealth. A Theory of Wages, Interest and Profits*, New York and London.

Conte, Michael A., and Jan Svejnar (1990), 'The Performance Effects of Employee Ownership Plans' in Blinder, Alan S. (ed.), *Paying for Productivity. A Look at the Evidence*, The Brookings Institution, Washington, D.C., pp. 143-182.

DeLong, J.B., and Lawrence H. Summers (1984), 'The changing cyclical variability of economic activity in the United States', National Bureau of Economic Research, *NBER Working Paper*, no. 1450, September.

Gordon, Robert J. (1988), 'Back to the future: European unemployment today viewed from America in 1939', *Brookings Papers on Economic Activity*, no. 1, pp. 271-304.

Hahn, Frank H., and Robert M. Solow (1986), 'Is Wage Flexibility a Good Thing?' in: Beckerman, Wilfred (ed.), *Wage Rigidity and Unemployment*, London, pp. 1-20.

Hashimoto, Masanori(1990), 'Employment and Wage Systems in Japan and their Implications for Productivity', in Blinder, Alan S. (ed.), *Paying for Productivity. A Look at the Evidence*, The Brookings Institution, Washington, D.C., pp. 245-296.

Husain, Aasim M. (1992), 'Private sector development in state-dominated economies', International Monetary Fund, unpublished Working Paper, October.

Layard, Richard, S. Nickell, and R. Jackman (1991), *Unemployment. Macroeconomic Performance and the Labor Market*, New York.

_____, _____ (1985), 'Unemployment, real wages, and aggregate demand in Europe, Japan and the United States', *Carnegie Rochester Series on Public Policy*, vol. 23, pp. 143-202.

_____ (1990), 'Wage bargaining and incomes policy: possible lessons for Eastern Europe', *Discussion Paper* no. 2, Centre for Economic Performance. London School for Economics and Political Science, London.

Levine, David, I., and Laura D'Andrea Tyson (1990), 'Participation, Productivity, and the Firm's Environment', in Blinder, Alan S. (ed.), *Paying for Productivity. A Look at the Evidence*, The Brookings Institution, Washington, D.C., pp. 183-244.

Organization of Economic Cooperation and Development (1992), *OECD Employment Outlook July 1992*. Organization for Economic Cooperation and

Development, Paris.

_____ (1990), *OECD Employment Outlook July 1990*. Organization for Economic Cooperation and Development, Paris.

Perraudin, William R.M. (1993), 'A framework for the analysis of pension and unemployment benefit reform in Poland', International Monetary Fund, University of Cambridge, Mimeographed.

Sachs, Jeffrey D. (1983), 'Real wages and unemployment in the OECD countries', *Brookings Papers on Economic Activity*, no. 1, pp. 255-289.

Solow, Robert M. (1990), *The Labor Market as a Social Institution*, Cambridge, Mass.

Summers, Lawrence H. (1990), *Understanding Unemployment*, Cambridge, Mass.

Weitzman, Martin L. (1986), 'The Simple Macroeconomics of Profit Sharing', in Beckerman, Wilfred (ed.), *Wage Rigidity and Unemployment*, London, pp. 171-200.

_____, and Douglas L. Kruse (1990), 'Profit Sharing and Productivity', in Blinder, Alan S. (ed.), *Paying for Productivity. A Look at the Evidence*, The Brookings Institution, Washington, D.C., pp. 95-142.

Section 3

Brainard, Lawrence J. (1991), 'Reform in Eastern Europe: Creating a capital market', *Federal Reserve Bank of Kansas City Economic Review* January/February, pp. 49-58

Brunner, B.K., and A.H. Meltzer (1968), 'Liquidity traps for money, bank credit, and interest rates', *Journal of Political Economy*, vol. 76, no.1, January/February, pp. 1-36.

Calvo, Guillermo A., M.S. Kumar, E. Borensztein, and P.R. Masson (1993), 'Financial sector reforms and exchange arrangements in Eastern Europe', International Monetary Fund, *Occasional Paper* no. 102, Washington D.C., February.

Campbell, Tim S. (1988), *Money and Capital Markets*, Glenview, Illinois, Boston, London.

Clark, J. A. (1988), 'Economies of scale and scope at depository financial institutions: a review of the literature', *Federal Reserve Bank of Kansas City Economic Review* September/October, pp. 16-33.

Corbett, Jenny, and Colin Mayer (1991), 'Financial reform in Eastern Europe: progress with the wrong model', *Oxford Review of Economic Policy*, vol. 7, no. 4, Winter, pp. 57-75.

Cukierman, Alex(1992), *Central Bank Strategy, Credibility, and Independence: Theory and Evidence*, Cambridge, Mass., and London .

Dornbusch, Rudiger, and Holger Wolf (1990), 'Monetary overhang and reforms in the 1940s, National Bureau of Economic Research, *NBER Working Paper*, no. 3456, October.

Fried, Joel, and Peter Howitt (1980), 'Credit rationing and implicit contract theory', *Journal of Money. Credit and Banking*, vol. 12, August, pp. 471-89.

Jarchow, Hans J. (1989), *Theorie und Politik des Geldes*, I. Geldtheorie, Goettingen.

McKinnon, Ronald (1973), *Money and Capital in Economic Development*, The Brookings Institution, Washington, D.C..

_____ (1988), 'Financial Liberalization in Retrospect: Interest Rate Policies in LDCs', in Ranis, Gustav, and T. Paul Schultz (eds.), *The State of Development Economics. Progress and Perspectives*, Cambridge, Mass. and Oxford, pp. 386-415.

Shaffer, S. (1988), 'A revenue-restricted cost study of 100 large banks', Federal Reserve Bank of New York, *Research Paper* no. 8806.

Siebke, Juergen (1972), 'An analysis of the german money supply process: the multiplier approach', *Supplements to Kredit und Kapital*, Heft 1, pp. 243-272.

Statistisches Bundesamt (1992), *Statistisches Jahrbuch 1992 für die Bundesrepublik Deutschland*, Wiesbaden.

Stigler, George (1965), 'Public regulation of the securities markets', *Journal of Business*, vol. 37, April, pp. 117-142.

Stiglitz, Joseph, E. (1989), 'Financial markets and development', *Oxford Review of Economic Policy*, vol. 5, no. 4, Winter, pp. 55-68.

_____ (1981), and Andrew Weiss, 'Credit rationing in markets with imperfect information', *American Economic Review*, vol. 71, June, pp. 393-410.

_____, _____ (1989), 'Banks as social accountants and screening devices and the general theory of credit rationing', *Essays in Monetary Economics in Honour of Sir John Hicks*, Oxford.

Tobin, James (1984), 'On the efficiency of the financial system', *Lloyds Bank Review*, no. 153, July, pp. 1-15.

_____ (1978), 'A proposal for international monetary reform', *Eastern Economic Journal*, vol. 4, pp. 153-159.

United States Department of Commerce (1992), United States National Income and Product Accounts Tables, *Survey of Current Business*, July.

van Horne, James C. (1985), 'Of financial innovations and excesses', *Journal of Finance*, vol. XL, no. 3, July, pp. 621-631.

Villanueva, Delano, and Abbas Mirakhor (1990), 'Strategies for financial reforms', *Staff Papers*, International Monetary Fund, vol. 37, no.3, pp. 509-536.

Section 4

Alesina, A. (1988), 'The End of Large Public Debts', in: Francesco Giavazzi, and Luigi Spaventa, *High Public Debt: The Italian Experience*, Cambridge, Mass..

_____, and Allen Drazen (1989), 'Why are stabilizations delayed?', National Bureau of Economic Research, *NBER Working Paper*, no. 3053, August.

Barro, Robert J.(1974), 'Are government bonds net wealth?', *Journal of Political Economy*, vol. 82, no. 6 , pp. 1095-1117.

_____ (1979), 'On the determination of public debt', *Journal of Political Economy*, vol. 87, pp. 940-71.

_____ (1989), 'The Ricardian approach to budget deficits', *Journal of Economic Perspectives*, vol. 3, no. 2, Spring, pp. 37-54.

Blanchard, Olivier J., (1990) 'Suggestions for a new set of fiscal indicators', *OECD Working Paper*, April.

_____ , Jean Claude Chouraqi and Robert P. Hagemann (1990), 'The sustainability of fiscal policy: new answers for an old question', *OECD Economic Studies*, no. 15, Autumn, pp. 7-36.

Blinder, Alan and Robert Solow (1974), 'Analytical foundations of fiscal policy', *Economics of Public Finance*, Washington, The Brookings Foundation.

Boskin, Michael J. (1978), 'Taxation, saving, and the rate of interest', *Journal of Political Economy*, vol. 86, Part 2, April, pp. S3-S27.

Buiter, Willem H. (1983), 'Measurement of the public sector deficit and its implications for policy evaluation and design', *Staff Papers*, International Monetary Fund, vol. 30, June, pp. 306-349.

_____ (1985), 'A guide to public sector debt and deficits', *Economic Policy*, vol. 1, November, pp. 14-79.

Chouraqui, J.-C., Robert Hagemann, and Nicola Sartor (1990), 'Indicators of fiscal policy: a reassessment', *Working Paper* no. 78, OECD, Department of Economics and Statistics.

Drazen, A. and Elhanan Helpman (1990), 'Inflationary consequences of anticipated macroeconomic policies', *The Review of Economic Studies*, vol. 57(1), no. 189, January, pp. 147-164.

Feldstein, Martin (1985), 'Debt and taxes in the theory of public finance', *Journal of Public Economics*, vol. 28, pp. 233-245.

Guidotti, Pablo E., and Manmohan S. Kumar (1991), 'Domestic public debt of externally indebted countries', International Monetary Fund, Occasional Paper no. 80, June.

Hambor, J. (1992), 'Issues in Eastern European social security reform', U.S. Treasury Department, Working Paper no. 9201, June.

Horne, Jocelyn (1991), 'Criteria of external sustainability', *European Economic Review*, vol. 35, pp. 1559-1574.

Kotlikoff, Laurence J. (1989), 'From deficit delusion to the fiscal balance rule: looking for an economically meaningful way to assess fiscal policy', National Bureau of Economic Research, *NBER Working Paper*, no. 2841, February.

Masson, Paul R. (1985), 'The sustainability of fiscal deficits', *Staff Papers*, International Monetary Fund, vol. 32, December, pp. 577-605.

Modigliani, Franco (1961), 'Long run implications of alternative fiscal policies and the burden of the national debt', *Economic Journal*, vol. 71, pp. 728-755.

McCallum, Bennett T. (1984), 'Are bond-financed deficits inflationary? A

Ricardian analysis', *Journal of Political Economy*, vol. 92, February, pp. 123-135.

Spaventa, Luigi (1987), 'The growth of public debt: sustainability, fiscal rules, and monetary rules', *Staff Papers*, International Monetary Fund, vol. 34, June, pp. 374-399.

Tanzi, Vito (1993), 'Fiscal policy and the economic restructuring of economies in transition', International Monetary Fund, unpublished Working Paper, March.

Tobin, James (1963), 'An Essay on the Principles of Debt Management', in Tobin, J. (ed.), *Fiscal and Debt Management Policies*, Englewood Cliffs, New Jersey: Prentice-Hall; reprinted in Tobin, J. (ed.), *Essays in Economics*, vol. 1, Amsterdam: North-Holland.

Zee, Howell H. (1988), 'The sustainability and optimality of government debt', *Staff Papers*, International Monetary Fund, vol. 35, December, pp. 658-685.